MW00628143

GOD'S
GRACE
IN THE VALLEY

CAM's policy is to use the King James Version of the Bible except in cases, such as in this book, when a few verses from another translation may be quoted for clarity. In such cases, the version used will be noted in the text.

Unattributed quotes and poems in this book by Faythelma Bechtel.

ISBN: 978-1-943929-25-2

Cover design and layout: Kristi Yoder

Printed in the USA

Published by:
TGS International
P.O. Box 355
Berlin, Ohio 44610 USA
Phone: 330-893-4828
Fax: 330-893-2305
www.tgsinternational.com

TGS001280

Meditations for grieving hearts

Faythelma Bechtel

Table of Contents

Part Two: Learning to Trust

Part Three: Looking Ahead

Dedication

In loving memory of my dear daughter, Sonya, who accepted the challenges of life and death with great fortitude and faith.

Preface

Like my first book of devotional meditations, *Reflections of God's Grace in Grief,* this book is born out of the tears, sorrow, and pain of my journeys with God and my loved ones through the valley of the shadow of death. As I reflect on those years, they seem like a mysterious nightmare, yet God's compassion and care have been a reality.

I cared for my mother for seven years in our home before she passed away on July 12, 2004. All through her life she had struggled with enormous mood swings. Today her disorder would be diagnosed as bipolar. Caring for her had been a colossal challenge that left me emotionally frazzled.

On February 14, 2005, our oldest daughter, Cynthia Bechtel Kropf, was diagnosed with inflammatory breast cancer, a rare, fast-growing cancer. Seven months later, she passed away, leaving her devoted husband and four children ages twelve to eighteen. She was buried on September 18, 2005, which would have been her forty-third birthday.

In August 2005, a month before our daughter's death, my husband was diagnosed with frontotemporal dementia. The doctor explained that he would regress into childhood and then become like an infant. He said that given Wilmer's strong, healthy body and his age of sixty-five, he could be an invalid for as long as twenty years. How difficult to accept this news! However, Wilmer's health and behavior deteriorated much more quickly than the doctor anticipated.

Life became a continual hassle and trauma. Changing my husband's diapers, cleaning up his messes, and finding him eating garbage, running off, and getting into everything that was not locked up were the events that made up my day.

Working through the loneliness, the crushed dreams, and then the grief of losing our daughter and seeing my husband deteriorate were almost more than my body and mind could handle. I was carrying a load I could not bear. My cry was, "Why, Lord, why can't I handle this? You said you would not give me more than I could bear. What is wrong with me?"

In 2007, we moved Wilmer to a care facility. I was forced to admit I could no longer do what I felt was my duty. However, Wilmer seemed to adjust well and was always smiling when I went to visit him. On April 21, 2008, just two days past his sixty-eighth birthday, Wilmer died of pneumonia, although dementia was the underlying cause of his death.

I was still walking the dark valley of widowhood when I received a life-changing call from Sonya, our youngest biological daughter. She called the week before Thanksgiving, in 2009. "I'm in the hospital, testing, finding nothing, but I have terrible pain." Her call came as a shock. I had no idea she had been sick.

I made an instant decision. "I'll be there as soon as I can get packed and get a ticket." The distance I would need to travel from Oregon to Missouri seemed insignificant compared to my daughter's pain.

I wrestled with God over fears about my daughter's condition. God couldn't be asking me to give up another dear daughter! Surely God would touch and heal her. However, she needed several surgeries on her intestine and colon. After the surgeries, we waited several days for the biopsy report to come back. One day four sober-faced doctors entered the hospital room and told us, "It is cancer." As soon as they disappeared from the room, I leaned over on the bed and wept. I thought I couldn't bear it. Why? Why? Why? Her three-year-old needed her. The rest of her family needed her. My finite human heart simply could not understand what God was doing.

Sonya took the news much more calmly than I, though she seemed in shock. But she chose to accept whatever God had planned for her. She was weak and slow in recovering from surgery. Still, she was ready to try some treatment. After a downhill struggle, Sonya passed away at her home in La Monte, Missouri, on May 12, 2010, three months before her forty-first birthday.

Only God knows the heart-wrenching pain of giving up yet another loved one. How often must I remind myself that my children are God's? They are gifts to me only as long as He deems necessary to fulfill His plan. In the midst of the pain, I had the peaceful joy of knowing that Sonya is fully recovered and resting in Christ's loving care, enjoying the presence of Jesus with her sister and father. How I long to see my loved ones up there!

Sonya's passing has wrung from my heart another collection of devotional meditations. Where could I go with a broken heart but to the Lord and His Word? Searching for comfort from God's Word, writing these meditations, and reading poetry and quotes from other hurting hearts have definitely been part of my healing process.

At the end of each devotional, I have provided questions that you may answer in your heart or record in your journal. Writing your responses provides a way to look back on them and observe your growth in the healing process.

My prayer is that these words will encourage and comfort your heart during your difficult journey through whatever dark valley you may be traversing. Life is never the same after losing a loved one, but life can be good again with God.

A fellow traveler,
Faythelma Bechtel

Acknowledgments

- A special thanks to my son Nolan, who preached many sermons—unknowingly for me—inspiring me, convicting me, directing my mind to pastures of peace and comfort, moving my focus from the reality of my humanity and my pain to the reality of God's greatness.

- I owe a special debt of gratitude to my daughter-in-law Annette for her ability to empathize and to offer words of encouragement. I thank God for her place in my heart.

- Most of all, I thank my Good Shepherd for walking with me through the dark valley. I thank Him for carrying me when my strength failed. I thank Him for His compassion and understanding and for the lessons learned in the valley.

Journaling Through the Valley

This devotional book with questions is intended to help you recognize and work through emotions that may be causing physical and spiritual illness. Whatever your loss or distress, we pray these meditations will increase your faith and reliance on the Good Shepherd.

Journaling is not so much about giving the right answers as it is about being honest with God, opening your heart and telling Him just how it is at the moment. God is interested in your feelings and cares about them. He is even more concerned about how you respond to the trials and pains that come into your life. His Word teaches you how to respond and deals with your attitude.

Grief has no orderly sequence. It enters the heart in chaotic confusion. One week you may be dealing with one emotion and another week a different one. One day you may have one fear and the next day face a different fear. One minute you may be in tears and the next minute you may be smiling. The emotional seesaw of grief is like riding the surging waves of the wild ocean.

Examine this brief list of losses and identify those that have been or are yours. When you think of your losses, think of your attitudes and responses; then always remember God's mercies and grace in your life. When the scales do not seem to balance, remember the greatest mercy and grace is still to come to the faithful—eternity with your Savior.

LOSSES

innocence
purity
caring parents
parent by abandonment
happy childhood
stable home
health
wealth
necessities
friends
security
physical ability
mental ability
love
sibling by death
parent by death
friend by death
child by death
companion by death
companion by divorce
material possessions

Whatever your loss, whatever your pain, you will find it beneficial and healing to journal as you journey through your dark valley. So if you desire healing, dig deep and be honest. Allow God to adjust your attitudes and responses. Here are a few pointers as you journal:

- Always write the date of entry. This will give you a reference point to look back at and see your progress.
- You do not need to work straight through this journal. If the next meditation does not seem appropriate for your present need, skip it and page on to something that fits your day.
- Never allow the lines given to limit your writing. Have a notebook ready for the overflow. Always list the page number of the devotional book on your notebook page.
- From meditation to meditation, you will find some of the same or nearly the same questions. As you work through this book, you may discover that your feelings about the same question change at different points and times.
- Use a concordance to find the needed Scriptures.
- At the end of each lesson write a statement of what you have learned or what meant the most to you in that meditation.

Emotions are a gift from God, never meant to rule your life, but meant to improve and broaden your experiences. The emotions that come with grief, sorrow, and loss are necessary to help you heal. They are not all wrong. What you do with the emotions is what makes them beneficial or harmful. For that reason you need to bring your thoughts into captivity and your feeling into control, without denying them or burying them.

Your knowledge of God and your relationship with Him will have the greatest bearing on how you deal with your grief. What do you know about the attributes of God? How have they helped you through life thus far? Do you have a head knowledge or a heart knowledge of the greatness of God? Studying the attributes of God, thinking on them, and thanking God for them, will help you work through your grief with a greater peace and assurance than you ever believed possible.

PART ONE
FACING THE PAIN

Guests

Pain knocked upon my door and said
That she had come to stay;
And though I would not welcome her
But bade her go away,

She entered in. Like my own shade
She followed after me,
And from her stabbing, stinging sword
No moment was I free.

And then one day another knocked
Most gently at my door.
I cried, "No, Pain is living here,
There is not room for more."

And then I heard His tender voice,
" 'Tis I, be not afraid."
And from the day He entered in,
What difference it has made!

For though He did not bid her leave,
(My strange, unwelcome guest)
He taught me how to live with her.
Oh, I had never guessed

That we could dwell so sweetly here,
My Lord and Pain and I,
Within this fragile house of clay
While years slip slowly by!

—Martha Snell Nicholson

Search Me

Search me, O God, and know my heart: try me, and know my thoughts: and see if there be any wicked way in me, and lead me in the way everlasting. Psalm 139:23–24

How fitting this prayer is when I am going through a trial. Trying times set my mind rolling, often in the wrong direction. Some days my thoughts recycle and recycle; some nights my mind will not shut off or quiet down. How can I survive this pain? How can I endure this heartbreak? How should I deal with this problem? Why is God letting this happen to me?

Recycling, for the most part, is beneficial and economical when it refers to bottles, cardboard, and paper. However, when it comes to recycling negative thoughts, the results are just the opposite—loss of sleep, energy, and creativity. This leads to stress, physical and mental pain, and spiritual distress. There is nothing beneficial or economical about recycling negative thoughts.

In a time of grief or trial, we have many questions and problems. But analyzing, scrutinizing, and dissecting them repeatedly will do us no good. Some questions have no sensible answers; trying to solve them muddles the brain. When the mind gets into the recycling mode, it is time to feed it some good thoughts to recycle. Here are some examples:

"How precious also are thy thoughts unto me, O God! how great is the sum of them! If I should count them, they are more in number than the sand: when I awake, I am still with thee" (Psalm 139:17–18).

"For I know the thoughts that I think toward you, saith the LORD, thoughts of peace, and not of evil, to give you an expected end" (Jeremiah 29:11).

"Commit thy works unto the LORD, and thy thoughts shall be established" (Proverbs 16:3).

"For my thoughts are not your thoughts, neither are your ways my ways, saith the LORD. For as the heavens are higher than the earth, so are my ways higher than your ways, and my thoughts than your thoughts" (Isaiah 55:8–9).

When life becomes complicated and agonizing, let's ask God to help us recycle thoughts of Him. It is not in man to understand all the purposes of God—that would make him equal with God.

Lord, help me to remember that my thoughts control my daily walk.

If God were small enough to be understood,
He would not be big enough to be trusted and worshiped.
—Evelyn Underhill

QUESTIONS

1. What thoughts am I recycling?
2. Am I suffering physically, spiritually, or emotionally due to recycled thoughts?
3. What are my unanswered questions?
4. Do I find it difficult to trust my unanswered questions into God's hands? Why or why not?

Am I a Light Reflector?

For thou wilt light my candle: the LORD my God will enlighten my darkness. Psalm 18:28

One evening I noticed all my solar lights were dark. I had been gone for seven weeks caring for my terminally ill daughter and her family of five. I glanced at the darkened lights another time and shook my head. Another job to add to my to-do list—new batteries for those lights. Being a widow was overwhelming at times like this. Just then, I felt as dark and useless as those extinguished solar lights!

Several weeks later we finally had a bright, sunny day. I enjoyed the afternoon working out in the sun. Later in the evening I was surprised to look out the patio door and see the solar lights shining brightly. The sun had turned the darkened lights into bright lights. There had been too many cloudy days—so many that the solar lights went dark because they had no light source.

A bulb lit in my brain. How like those solar lights I had become! During the gloomy days we had gone through, dark thoughts had spread through my mind. Ominous feelings flooded my spirit. My heart throbbed for my daughter who had recently been diagnosed with cancer. I had spent too much time dwelling in the cloudy darkness, not allowing myself enough time to receive the SONshine. How dark and hopeless I felt.

I looked at my reflection in the mirror. I looked shadowed. No one could have found a trace of light in my face. "Oh, God, forgive me," I prayed. "I do not reflect your light. I need you to light my candle! Oh, God, give me some light to reflect."

How I need the SONshine of God's love, comfort, and hope! Only His light can brighten the thoughts of my mind and the feelings of my heart.

It's easy to trust when the sun's shining bright,
And all is at peace on the pathway of life.

In times of deep trouble then where do we stand?
Does faith keep on singing or sink in the sand?

The God who sends sunshine will also send pain,
There's never a rainbow appears without rain.

Our trust in His Word should be steady and true;
There's never a trial He won't see us through.

—author unknown

Steps to get God's light back into my life:

- Confess my feelings and release them to God.
- Follow the light of what I know is right.
- Remember that I am not alone. Others have walked the dark valley of disappointment and pain before I have, and many more will walk it after me.
- Turn my focus away from my feelings to the facts of God's sovereignty, goodness, and love.

QUESTIONS

1. What emotions are making it dark for me right now?
2. Looking at the above steps, where am I moving forward, and where am I stuck?
3. In what ways am I trying to reflect God's light?

Time Out

And he said unto them, Come ye yourselves apart into a desert place, and rest a while: for there were many coming and going, and they had no leisure so much as to eat. Mark 6:31

Dealing with grief and pain is hard work; we need to take time out!

- Take time to rest often.
- Make a conscious effort to relax.
- Practice deep breathing. Inhale deeply through your nose and exhale slowly through your mouth.
- Work on a picture puzzle, do a crossword or Sudoku puzzle, knit, work in the shop, or do whatever helps you relax. It is amazing how much a short break will energize you.
- Go for a brisk walk.
- Pull some weeds in the garden.
- Send a card to someone the Lord brings to your mind.

When our thoughts are stuck in a rut or our self-talk is taking us down the wrong road, we should reprogram our thoughts with Bible verses, such as the following:

- "Rest in the Lord" (Psalm 37:7).
- "Fret not thyself" (Psalm 37:7).
- "I will trust and not be afraid" (Isaiah 12:2).
- "Commit thy way unto the Lord" (Psalm 37:5).
- "Be still and know that I am God" (Psalm 46:10).
- "Stand still, and see the salvation of the LORD" (Exodus 14:13).
- "God is our refuge" (Psalm 46:1).
- "I will lay me down in peace" (Psalm 4:8).
- "The Lord is my shepherd" (Psalm 23:1).

Many people find it helpful to list verses that speak to their personal needs.

These verses can be written on index cards and posted where they will be seen throughout the day.

When we are grieving, we should not try to jump right back into life, pretending things are normal. We must take time with other hurting family members, take time to listen to God, and allow time for our bodies and emotions to heal.

QUESTIONS

1. Do I feel guilty when I take time to recharge ?
2. Have I been focusing too much on doing rather than being?
3. Is my time of tribulation teaching me that there are many things more important than the daily grind of doing what needs to be done with little fulfillment?
4. How am I building relationships during this time of stress?

Disappointment Is God's Appointment

As the hart panteth after the water brooks, so panteth my soul after thee, O God. My soul thirsteth for God, for the living God: when shall I come and appear before God? My tears have been my meat day and night, while they continually say unto me, Where is thy God? Psalm 42:1–3

Pain in the heart and tears in the eyes make a thirsty mouth and a panting heart that problem-free living could never create. That is one of God's appointments for disappointments. Actually, it is the fundamental reason for life's disappointments. A thirst for God is the only railroad that will take us out of this sin-cursed world into His heavenly kingdom.

When we are happy and comfortable, we usually do not seek to know God. When life is more sun than rain, we fool ourselves into believing that life is always going to be wonderful. We do not feel a need for God.

It is sad that we generally use God as a Band-Aid or a 911 call when we need Him. Sometimes He even needs to pile on the disappointments before we think seriously about the direction of our lives. His will is to turn disappointments into appointments—means of accomplishing His purposes.

- Disappointment is God's appointment to teach me patience.
- Disappointment is God's appointment to teach me trust.
- Disappointment is God's appointment to increase my faith.
- Disappointment is God's appointment for me to develop a meaningful personal relationship with Him.
- Disappointment is God's appointment for me to acknowledge His sovereignty.
- Disappointment is God's appointment for me to surrender to His plan for my life.
- Disappointment is God's appointment for me to accept my circumstances and deal with the pain they bring.
- Disappointment is God's appointment to teach me to reach out and touch someone with love.

Larry Crabb describes our tendency to be in denial about our pain: "There is incredible resistance in Christian circles to owning internal pain. Even a glance in the direction of discouragement and fear violate our idea of what a victorious Christian should be doing. Many Christian people have been trained to deny that they hurt."[1]

When we deny our hurt, we fail to acknowledge our thirst. Only an awareness of our thirst and the pursuit of God can turn our disappointments into God's appointments.

QUESTIONS

1. What disappointments am I dealing with presently?
2. What were some major disappointments in my past?
3. How have disappointments been God's appointments in my life?
4. Karol Truman said, "Feelings buried alive never die."[2] What feelings have I denied for many years or am presently burying? What should I do with them now?
5. When life was fairly smooth and without major problems, how did I function? What was my relationship with God? What was my relationship with my loved ones?
6. How has my present pain helped me build a loving relationship with God? What am I thirsting for in my human relationships?

Am I a Hypocrite?

Woe unto you, scribes and Pharisees, hypocrites! Matthew 23:14

Jesus hated the hypocrisy He saw in the religious leaders of His day, and He reproves and denounces it in His followers today. Am I ever like the Pharisees in my feelings and expressions? Whose image am I building? Whose character am I promoting—mine or Christ's?

- Woe to me when I tell others what to do, but fail to do it myself.
- Woe to me when I choose the chief seats, receive glory for my position, and desire to be noticed in public, but ignore my loved ones—those who do the most for me.
- Woe to me when my hypocrisy keeps men out of God's kingdom.
- Woe to me if I devour the widow's reputation in private, yet make long prayers for her in public.
- Woe to me if I deceive and backbite to make a proselyte to my name and honor.
- Woe to me when I value the opinions of others more than honest, loving relationships at home and abroad.
- Woe to me when I keep the "public front" glowing and kind, while on the home front I am thoughtless and merciless.
- Woe to me when I have my priorities all mixed up, for God will come with some uncomfortable trials and help me sort them into correct order.
- Woe to me when I talk sweetly to a person's face and harshly behind his back.
- Woe to me if I put on a front of handling my grief well when my heart is full of tension.
- Woe to me if I "dress right," "smile right," "say it right," and "do it right," while inside my heart little is right. I am as the blind Pharisees to whom Jesus said, "Cleanse first that which is within the cup and platter, that the outside of them may be clean also" (Matthew 23:26).

How often do I find myself hiding among the scribes, Pharisees, and hypocrites? Jesus had some sharp words for these groups.

O Lord, forgive my pharisaic attitudes and judgments. If and when I am right, help me not to dwell on this fact, but help me to be merciful as you are merciful.

Shakespeare's character Jaques said, "All the world's a stage, and all the men and women merely players" (*As You Like It*, 2.7.138–139). *Lord, preserve me from this mentality that I often embrace unconsciously.* God does not want or need "performers." He wants genuine dwellers in the truth—those who believe and live their faith in everyday life.

QUESTIONS

1. What woes might Jesus say to me?
2. Have I made some rash judgments or said some harsh words? How have I taken care of my wrongs?
3. In what area of life am I most tempted to play the hypocrite?
4. Do I protect my personal image more than the image of Christ?

Not Indispensable

It is vain for you to rise up early, to sit up late, to eat the bread of sorrows: for so he giveth his beloved sleep. Psalm 127:2

On the verge of a nervous breakdown, a middle-aged man went to the doctor. He told the doctor how much work he had to do and how he was the only one who could do it. This was the doctor's prescription:

- Take off two hours of every working day and spend time cultivating traits and attitudes that will keep you young.
- Take off half a day every week and wander through a cemetery. Look at the gravestones of those who thought the work of the world rested on their shoulders. Meditate on the fact that when your body lies six feet under, the world will continue turning—you were not indispensable after all.
- Then sit down among the tombstones and quote these verses:
  - "Boast not thyself of tomorrow; for thou knowest not what a day may bring forth" (Proverbs 27:1).
  - "The voice said, Cry. And he said, What shall I cry? All flesh is grass, and all the goodliness thereof is as the flower of the field: the grass withereth, the flower fadeth: because the spirit of the LORD bloweth upon it: surely the people is grass. The grass withereth, the flower fadeth: but the word of our God shall stand for ever" (Isaiah 40:6–8).

Guess what? The patient got well, and his friends and business associates liked him better than before. He was a changed man. A different inner look gave him a different outer look.

Being irresponsible or being too responsible are ditches on either side of the road of life. We need to avoid either extreme. Too often I find myself carrying more responsibility than God ever intended me to carry. I wonder if God ever looks down on me and says, ***Who does she think she is? A proud, independent, superwoman? Here I am, waiting to carry her burdens and share her heartaches, and she plunges on in blind helplessness, thinking everything is her responsibility!***

Forgive me, Lord! My struggling strength falters. My insurgent independence is a flop. Why do I keep pushing ahead in my own strength?

So now, you must put me through the same lesson again.

When I am weak, then I am strong.

When I give in, you walk beside me.

When I give out, your arms uphold me.

When I give up, you pick me up and carry me.

QUESTIONS

1. Am I adding to my stress by taking too much responsibility?
2. Am I struggling with an independent spirit?
3. How does God want me to feel about the pain in my life?
4. In what ways has God shown me I am not indispensable?
5. Has my emotional stress resulted in physical or spiritual problems?

Tithing Our Grief

Bring ye all the tithes into the storehouse, that there may be meat in mine house, and prove me now herewith, saith the LORD of hosts, if I will not open you the windows of heaven, and pour you out a blessing, that there shall not be room enough to receive it. Malachi 3:10

I feel barren—except for imaginations; dried up—except for tears; unproductive—except for sighs. I do not want to be that way, but the trials of life seem to drain all fruitfulness out of me. Grief can leave me shriveled and useless. It can even cause me to hurt other people. Someone said, "Hurting people hurt people."

What can I do to keep from shriveling up, from being useless, and from hurting others? In these verses in Malachi, God said in essence, "Present your tithes to me and I will bless you and make you a blessing!"

What tithes? Tears! I will bring my tears to the Lord and He will put them in His bottle. "Thou tellest my wanderings: put thou my tears into thy bottle: are they not in thy book? When I cry unto thee, then shall mine enemies turn back: this I know; for God is for me" (Psalm 56:8–9). I have the assurance that when I cry to God, my enemies of fear, anger, and doubt will turn back.

I will bring to God my tithe of difficulties and pain. "In the day of my trouble I will call upon thee: for thou wilt answer me" (Psalm 86:7). "He shall call upon me, and I will answer him: I will be with him in trouble; I will deliver him, and honour him" (Psalm 91:15).

Now comes the hard one. I will bring to God my tithe of praise and thanksgiving. Even in the darkest night there is a reason to give thanks. "And he hath put a new song in my mouth, even praise unto our God: many shall see it, and fear, and shall trust in the LORD. Blessed is that man that maketh the LORD his trust" (Psalm 40:3–4).

When I shrivel, become useless, or hurt others, I am robbing God of the worship I owe Him. He has some severe words for those who rob Him of His dues: "Will a man rob God? Yet ye have robbed me. But ye say, Wherein have we robbed thee? In tithes and offerings. Ye are cursed with a curse: for ye have robbed me, even this whole nation" (Malachi 3:8–9).

I must remember—when I rob God, I am also robbing myself. Times of trial and grief are times to seek God, not ignore Him. These are times to give to

God, not to take away from Him; times to trust and wait on God, not doubt and question Him.

QUESTIONS

1. What are ten things for which I am thankful right now?
2. What are some tithes I can offer God in this trial?
3. In what ways might I be robbing God?
4. What does giving to God and others do for me?

Moving Out of the Shadow of Grief

In the day of my trouble I sought the Lord: my sore ran in the night, and ceased not: my soul refused to be comforted. Will the Lord cast off for ever? and will he be favourable no more? Is his mercy clean gone for ever? doth his promise fail for evermore? Hath God forgotten to be gracious? hath he in anger shut up his tender mercies? Selah. And I said, This is my infirmity: but I will remember the years of the right hand of the most High. I will remember the works of the LORD: surely I will remember thy wonders of old. I will meditate also of all thy work, and talk of thy doings. Psalm 77:2, 7–12

"You cannot move ahead if you just stand still." I found this quote posted at an ironic place—at the airport beside a moving walkway, the only place you *can* stand still and yet move ahead!

The writer of this psalm seems to have been standing still. Perhaps he had even sat down in the shadow of his grief. He refused to be comforted. At times during grief it feels good not to be comforted. However, woe to us if we refuse God's comfort, which we need so badly.

When we refuse comfort or sit down in the shadow of our grief, our lives can become stagnant and smelly. When Satan tempts us to stand still, convincing us that God is the cause of our troubles, it is time to play "Memory," reflecting on how God has helped us in the past. It also is time to remember we are walking *through* the valley of the shadow; it is neither our intent nor God's plan for us to stay there.

Let's think on, meditate on, and remember God's merciful dealings with His people in the Bible. Let's think on God's changeless character and our own experiences of God's faithfulness—the prayers He answered, the sins He pardoned, and the strength, peace, and grace He gave each day. Remembering God's faithfulness can help us move ahead with confidence and hope.

When we suffer an eclipse of joy like the one recorded in this psalm, we need to check if we are standing still or sitting in the shadow of our grief. Living in the darkness of sorrow is cold and demotivating. It brings us to a stunted dead end.

To move out of the shadow of our grief, we must remember God's favors, His promises, and His wonderful doings. Look for the sunrise and the sunset. Watch for His rainbows of promise. Gaze at the stars. Smell deeply the rose and feel its velvet petals. Observe the fluttering butterfly. Listen for the buzz of the bees. Hear the songs of the mockingbird. See the wonder of life in a child's eyes. Hear the happy giggle of children at play and you will come to life again. You will see God's greatness and goodness, and you will thank Him, for you are walking out from under the shade of grief.

Do not sit in the shadow of your grief.

QUESTIONS

1. Do I really want to find comfort or does my grief feel good?
2. Am I comfortable sitting on the sidelines as a passive spectator while life goes on?
3. What are some things I can do to help bring joy back into my life?

Thanksgiving

I will sing of mercy and judgment: unto thee, O LORD, will I sing. Psalm 101:1

When my first daughter died, I attended grief classes with a friend. One exercise in class was to write a list every day of five things for which we were thankful. We were not allowed to repeat something we had mentioned on a previous list. This was a very simple but difficult assignment.

Here's an example of what I wrote one day.

Five things for which I am thankful today:

- A note from a friend
- Rain
- A caring family
- Breath for this new day
- An encouraging phone call

My thanks were simplistic at first. It was difficult to get my mind thinking in terms of thankfulness. I was shocked that I had such a difficult time finding things for which I was thankful. Gradually my "thanks" came from a deeper place inside me. My thanks for one day was: *I am thankful for strength to work in my flower garden.* Several weeks later: *Thank you for helping me see my anger toward you concerning Cynthia's death.* Weeks later: *Thank you for our family being together and for a time of sharing roses and memories of Cynthia.*

Why is being thankful important? The Scriptures tell us often to "give thanks." Thanksgiving helps us recognize and remember the mercies of God. When we are thankful, we will focus on what we have rather than what we have lost.

Singing is a part of being thankful. Thankfulness increases our desire to sing. We can sing without being thankful, but it is difficult to be thankful without singing.

Singing was difficult after my losses. Some songs brought me immediately to tears. Others I could not sing, but I determined to sing what I could. I really did not want to be like someone I knew who did not sing for several years after a loss. Singing can be a means of finding healing.

Praise songs, songs of creation, and songs of God's goodness lift the spirit and promote a positive attitude. *Help me, Lord, to sing of your mercies at least once a day!* Singing not only makes me feel better, but it encourages those near me—and best of all, it pleases God.

QUESTIONS

1. Can I list five things for which I am thankful?
2. Could my situation be worse in any way than it is?
3. In what ways has God shown me mercy?
4. What does singing do for me?

Freedom in Forgiveness

Lord, how oft shall my brother sin against me,
and I forgive him? till seven times? Matthew 18:21

Peter was troubled about the matter of forgiving. We can only surmise the nature of the wrong that had been committed against him. Perhaps it was a power struggle with some of the other disciples. Maybe they had mocked him for his forwardness in answering questions. Under the law, forgiving three times was all that was required, so Peter must have felt very magnanimous in his question.

"How oft shall my brother sin against me, and I forgive him? till seven times?" (Matthew 18:21). He was willing to forgive four more times than was required. Surely Jesus would be satisfied with his offer.

How did Jesus answer Peter? "I say not unto thee, Until seven times: but, Until seventy times seven" (Matthew 18:22). In other words, the Lord told Peter and the rest of the disciples that we must forgive always. We can never come to the point of refusing to forgive, regardless of whether or not forgiveness is sought by the offender. A person with a humble, childlike spirit will forgive any number of times and will not keep a record of offenses.

"If ye forgive not men their trespasses, neither will your Father forgive your trespasses," Jesus told His followers another time (Matthew 6:15). In the parable of the unforgiving servant, Jesus shows the power of forgiveness (Matthew 18:23–34). He is the King who has forgiven a debt we could never repay in a lifetime. He showed us mercy when there was no mercy to be found anywhere else in the world. His forgiveness has given me, His child, an eternal inheritance. Yet often I forget the price He paid to forgive me and the power of His forgiveness, and I demand justice from my fellowmen. How often do I forget the countless times He has forgiven me, and I strike back at a brother with an unforgiving lash?

When I refuse to forgive someone, I make myself a slave to that person. The very sight of that person rankles me. My stomach ties in knots when I am near him. I am in bondage to him. Only forgiveness will release me from my bondage.

Forgiveness is a matter of choice, not feelings.
When you allow yourself to brood, you have not truly forgiven.
—Corrie Ten Boom

Forgiveness is priceless, yet much cheaper than resentment.

Forgiveness saves the expense of anger, the cost of hatred,
and the waste of despondency.

—Hannah More

QUESTIONS

1. The more I realize the weakness and failures of my humanness, the brighter shines the mercy and forgiveness of God. What is wrong when I do not feel mercy and forgiveness for others?
2. In what areas am I struggling with forgiveness?
3. What are the possible repercussions of not forgiving?
4. Do I feel a person must ask for forgiveness before I can forgive?
5. Why am I duty-bound to always forgive?

Grace Enough

But he giveth more grace. Wherefore he saith, God resisteth the proud, but giveth grace unto the humble. Submit yourselves therefore to God. Resist the devil, and he will flee from you. James 4:6-7

Alice was not about to expose the pain in her heart to anyone. She would be heroic, brave, and calm at the funeral. She did not want anyone to see her cry. Her faith in God would see her through this horrific experience. No one would ever find out that her heart felt like a hole had been blasted through the middle of it.

In her stubborn self-sufficiency, Alice failed to realize that God gives grace to those who are humble enough to accept it. Why do I, like Alice, steel myself against a show of emotions? Why do I put on a front? Why do I want people to believe I have a strong faith? Because I am PROUD!

I need to stop before God periodically and check how I am dealing with my grief. Am I stuffing my emotions inside a breaking heart? Do I ignore my feelings of anger, fear, and doubt because I think such feelings make God upset with me? Do I allow myself time to sit and think about my loss and face it in honesty? Do I allow myself to cry and feel the pain? Am I reaching out to God for grace and strength? Do I pray and read God's Word, seeking strength and guidance through the dark valley?

God gives more grace to those who are humble enough to ask for it. If I am not humble enough to ask for God's grace, I will not be humble enough to accept it. Is it not pride that keeps me plunging blindly through the valley, causing me to forget that my ways are not His ways? Is it not pride that covers reality with pretense? Is it not pride that refuses to acknowledge my weakness and ask for His strength?

When I am truly humble I will:

- Trust God to handle my affairs—even in the dark.
- Recognize my weakness, inability, and lack of foresight.
- Be still and rest in God's goodness.
- Accept whatever God sends as a discipline of grace.

- Allow the trial of my faith to bring glory to God.
- Ask God for grace, knowing I cannot survive without it.
- Accept my humanity and thank God for His sovereignty.

God wants to write a story of hope, goodness, and grace in my life for others to see. Am I willing?

QUESTIONS

1. Am I asking for God's grace in my life?
2. Am I accepting God's grace in my life?
3. Grace can be defined as the ability to do things God's way. How is God's grace showing in my life?
4. How might I be struggling with pride in the way I am dealing with my loss?

Burdens or Wings?

But they that wait upon the LORD shall renew their strength; they shall mount up with wings as eagles; they shall run, and not be weary; and they shall walk, and not faint. Isaiah 40:31

In her devotional book, *Streams in the Desert,* Lettie Cowman tells a fable about the way the birds acquired their wings.

> God first made them without wings. Then God made wings, put them down before the wingless birds, and said to them, "Come, take up these burdens and bear them."
>
> The birds had lovely plumage and sweet voices. They could sing, and their feathers gleamed in the sunshine, but they could not soar in the air. They hesitated at first when bidden to take up the burdens that lay at their feet, but soon they obeyed, and taking up the wings in their beaks, they laid them on their shoulders to carry them.
>
> For a while, the load seemed heavy and hard to bear, but presently, as they went on carrying the burdens, folding them over their hearts, the wings grew fast to their little bodies, and soon they discovered how to use them, and the wings lifted them into the air.
>
> Like the birds in this parable, we are wingless, and our duties and trials are the pinions God made to lift us up and carry us heavenward. We look at our burdens and heavy loads, and we shrink from them; but as we lift them and bind them about our hearts, they become wings, enabling us to rise and soar toward God.[3]

There is no burden that, if we lift it cheerfully and bear it with love in our hearts, will not become a blessing to us. God means our trials to be our helpers; to refuse to bend our shoulders to receive a load is to decline a new opportunity for growth.[4]

—J.R. Miller

As I learn to wait upon God, He will work through the trials, bringing me to a place where I can thank Him for the pain that seems so heavy now. One day that pain will become the wings that carry me toward my heavenly goal.

For though He prove our patience,
And to the utmost prove,
Yet all his dispensations
Are faithfulness and love.[5]
—J. J. Given

QUESTIONS

1. God never has a problem; He has a plan and a purpose. I can fit into His plan and purpose by accepting what I do not understand. What things am I trying to accept that I do not understand?
2. What does it mean to "wait upon the Lord"?
3. When we lose hope, we lose patience. In what areas of my life have I lost hope and patience?
4. What burdens have turned into blessings in my life?

Divine Sympathy

The Lord is gracious, and full of compassion;
slow to anger, and of great mercy. Psalm 145:8

God extends divine sympathy to me whenever I need it. He never misunderstands me. He knows better than I do how and why I feel and react the way I do. He never makes fun of me or ignores me. He never condones self-pity, however; He offers companionship, courage, and hope.

Through His divine sympathy, the Lord feels my pain in His heart. He dries my tears and gives me a hug of courage to go on through the day. Just when I feel like I am going under, His right hand reaches out and lifts me from the depths of sorrow. In moments of repose, I catch my breath and pray. He replaces my panic with peace.

Thank you, Lord, for your gracious compassion and divine sympathy. Give me a heart that cares for and shares in the pain of other hurting hearts. Fill me with your compassion. Help me to make the most of each moment, for life is precious.

There is Someone who always walks beside me
And He will leave me—never!
He is my Friend and I am His,
Forever and forever.

—Leona Choy

Make the most of your moments;
Don't let them fade or fly past,
Unnoticed, unused, or ignored;
For other hearts are downcast.

Some need a smile or a hug,
Some need you to look their way.
Some need an encouraging word;
Some need you to stop and pray.

Some need you to cry with them,
Some want to share their cares.
Make the most of your moments now;
Be that special angel unawares!

QUESTIONS

1. In what ways does divine sympathy differ from human sympathy?
2. Have there been times when I did not show appropriate sympathy?
3. Since my valley experience, am I using my moments differently? If so, how? If not, why not?

Touching the Lives of Others

How long shall I take counsel in my soul, having sorrow in my heart daily? how long shall mine enemy be exalted over me? Psalm 13:2

How long shall the enemy, grief, crush my heart? I know not how long, but it must not be too long, or I will sink into despair and not learn the lessons God is trying to teach me. Grief becomes an enemy only when I move away from God. When I allow God to direct me through my sorrow, my pain can become an amazing learning experience.

Sorrow can ennoble, purify, and strengthen us. In sorrow's silence and loneliness, in its self-examination and penitence, its pain and patience, the loveliest Spirit fruit appears. In learning to bear our own burden, we also learn to bear the burdens of others.

Was John Bunyan put in the Bedford jail on his own account or for the world's benefit? Was John Milton blind for his own sake or for England's? Was Fanny Crosby's blindness the result of the doctor's malpractice or God's foreknowledge?

How could *Pilgrim's Progress, Paradise Lost,* or hundreds of our hymns and works of literature have been produced, except by these people becoming partakers in suffering and consolation? "And our hope of you is stedfast, knowing, that as ye are partakers of the sufferings, so shall ye be also of the consolation" (2 Corinthians 1:7).

Suffering is never a one-person event. My suffering may be like an irrigation ditch that passes on nourishment to all the fields around it. On the other hand, my suffering can become as a ditch filled with herbicide, spreading poison everywhere. How am I accepting and dealing with what God has allowed in my life?

When I share in Christ's sufferings, I can also share in His consolation. What a challenge! How did Christ suffer? "Not my will, but thine, be done" (Luke 22:42). "Father, forgive them; for they know not what they do" (Luke 23:34). Christ's focus in His suffering was all about others, not Himself. What is my suffering all about? Am I sharing in Christ's suffering and in His consolation?

I am certain my sorrow will never reach out and benefit millions as Bunyan's jail experience helped him reach out, but it *will* touch other lives—for better or for worse. *O Lord, make my suffering count for your glory!*

It is the capacity to suffer which is the
dignity and glory of our nature.

QUESTIONS

1. How has some hurting person been a blessing to me?
2. In what ways has my sorrow not been a one-person event? How has it affected my family and friends?
3. What are some of the burdens I need to bear because of my loss?
4. What are the burdens only God can bear?
5. What is the promise in 2 Timothy 2:12, and what is the warning?

Shadow Grief

I will love thee, O LORD, my strength. Psalm 18:1

Have you ever blocked a pain until suddenly you could block it no longer? That happened to me one evening when I was having pain in my jaws. I went to brush my teeth, and suddenly realized how sore my jaws were. I found I could hardly stand to brush my teeth. I found my tube of pain-relieving toothpaste, gently applied it to my teeth, and left it there for a few minutes, hoping it would ease the pain. Soon I realized I had been clamping my teeth all evening and likely all afternoon, judging by the pain in my jaw and teeth.

That evening I had a very difficult time settling down. The next morning, after a bad night, I was weepy, nervous, and dealing with panic. My blood pressure was high. It had been stable before. *Whatever is going on? What is wrong with me?* I was unmotivated, hurting all over—my stomach ached, my head throbbed, my heart beat irregularly, and I felt incredibly sad. Sadness was normal with me since my second daughter had died the previous month, but all this was much worse than normal.

Finally I looked at the calendar—the seventeenth. Then I found my daughter's funeral program and was reminded that her funeral had been on the seventeenth. The very lengthy viewing had been on the evening of the sixteenth. Now I understood all my physical and emotional problems! I was dealing with "shadow grief." I had experienced it often in the months following my first daughter's death and my husband's death, but somehow this time it had caught me off guard.

All at once I realized how strong God's arm had been the night of the viewing and the day of the funeral. Since His arm was so strong then, it would surely be strong now. Having an explanation for what was going on brought a lot of relief.

I have learned that shadow grief is very real. It often comes on birthdays, anniversaries, holidays, death dates, or funeral dates. However, it does not come to everyone. It is described as "the intense sadness that overcomes us when least expected, like a shadow from the past that darkens the day, the moment or the mood . . . This reliving of grief may occur at any time, usually at the most unexpected moments, and comes and goes for a lifetime. While shadow grief is often associated with mothers whose children have died, anyone can experience this type of grief burst."[6] When we recognize it, it is much easier to deal with. God's arm, which upheld us before, is present now and will uphold us again.

> Each substance of a grief hath twenty shadows.
> —William Shakespeare

> God is too great to be withstood, too just to do wrong, too good to delight in any one's misery. We ought, therefore, to quietly submit to his dispensations as the very best.
> —Bishop Wilson

QUESTIONS

1. How have I experienced shadow grief?
2. What are some things I might do to prepare myself for shadow grief?
3. How has God helped me in the past?
4. Death is not the only experience that brings shadows. An accident, abuse, separation, or another traumatic experience may cause shadows of grief and pain. What shadows have I experienced from traumas? What emotions have I had to deal with?

Contentment

But godliness with contentment is great gain. 1 Timothy 6:6

Where can I find contentment? God alone is my source of contentment because He is my—

Comforter
Only Savior
Necessary Route
Trusted Shepherd
Eternal Hope
Never-Failing Friend
Tender Companion
Merciful Father
Ever-Present Help
Nurturing Guide
Thorough Teacher

When life seems all is losing;
That's the time to do some choosing.

It's the time to recognize
Some blessings may come in disguise.

Your hurts, trials, sorrow, pain
Prepare your heart for Christ to reign.

He'll be your Friend and your Stay,
He'll be your Hope, your Light, your Way.

So be content—it is great gain,
To dwell where He alone doth reign.

When I get that aching, restless unhappiness in my heart, I now recognize it as discontentment—that feeling of dissatisfaction with my lot in life, with my trials, with my valley experience, with my life in general. This feeling is the danger signal that reminds me not to fall into Satan's trap of taking for granted the great power, love, and care of my almighty God. When I become discontented, I can easily fall into the pit of self-pity. My focus must shift away from myself and my pain to appreciate Christ, His blessings, and the challenges to grow more like Him. Changing my focus is not always easy, but when I choose to do so, my Comforter always shows Himself strong on my behalf.

God tells us, "Be content with such things as you have." When we practice the following steps to contentment, given by E.B. Pusey, we find the peace and joy God planned for us.

- Never allow yourself to complain of anything, not even of the weather.
- Never picture yourself under any circumstance in which you are not.
- Never compare your lot in life with that of another.
- Never allow yourself to dwell on the wish that this or that were otherwise than what is. God Almighty loves you better and more wisely than you love yourself.
- Never dwell on the morrow. Remember that it is God's, not yours. Often, the heaviest part of sorrow is to look forward to it. The Lord will provide.

QUESTIONS

1. Am I content with my relationship with God? With my family?
2. Am I content with what God is doing in my life right now?
3. Do I show signs of discontentment? What would I desire to have changed?
4. What is the best way to remedy discontentment?

Charity

Now the end of the commandment is charity out of a pure heart, and of a good conscience, and of faith unfeigned. 1 Timothy 1:5

Lord, I am already wounded. Why do I have to be shot down, and why by a Christian friend? I don't fit, I don't belong, I'm not needed. They haven't time for me. I am just in the way. She always ignores me. Why do I have to be the one reaching out, speaking first, taking the initiative to be friendly? I am the one who is hurting.

Such are the thoughts that can pass through the love-starved, lonely, grieving heart and mind. Does it sound like a bad case of self-pity? Maybe, but it is the groanings of a hurting heart trying to find a new normal. Grief leaves one feeling totally abnormal, uprooted, disheveled, confused, and sometimes unloved and unneeded.

Time, effort, and the work of the Spirit help the hurting heart and mind to get the focus off the pain and on what really matters. What really matters is that "the end of the commandment is charity." Charity loves God first and our fellowmen next. This love flows out of a pure heart, a heart free of selfishness, pride, and evil imaginations. This love springs from a good conscience. Keeping a good conscience requires effort under the best conditions; a person in grief needs to clear his conscience even more carefully and more often. A clouded conscience often causes one to misjudge, overreact, or feel hurt.

How often I need to plead for forgiveness! How often I cry out, *O God, please help me to think right. Help me to not misjudge. Please help me to not hurt someone else. There is already so much pain in this loss that I certainly do not want to add more. May your love help keep my conscience clear.*

This love comes from faith unfeigned—a true, honest, sincere faith. Faith supplies the power for victory. When my faith is unfeigned, then God is real to me. I can count on His power, His mercy, and His grace to carry me through any difficulty.

When life's inner springs flow out of a pure heart, a good conscience, and an honest faith, I can be certain my life is creating a good atmosphere for healthy personal relationships. That does not mean that I will be at the top of everybody's list of best liked or most appreciated people. However, I will be on God's list of those obeying the end of the commandment, which is charity.

> [Charity] beareth all things, believeth all things,
> hopeth all things, endureth all things.
> 1 Corinthians 13:7

QUESTIONS

1. Love is the best way to find victory over hurting others and being hurt. How can I share love with difficult people?
2. Am I uncomfortable with people who are hurting? Why?
3. How can I grow in compassion and reaching out to others who hurt?
4. What are some reasons I think people avoid me when I am hurting?
5. Should I expect everyone to "feel" for me when I am hurting?

Psalm 63

O God, thou art my God; early will I seek thee: my soul thirsteth for thee, my flesh longeth for thee in a dry and thirsty land, where no water is. Psalm 63:1

Chrysostom, an early church father, said of Psalm 63, "It was decreed and ordained by the primitive fathers that no day should pass without the public singing of this Psalm."[7] If we would read and think on it every day, it certainly would improve our spirits, shed light during troubled times, and brighten our path through the dark valley. So, let's lift up our heads and hearts, read Psalm 63, and be strengthened in faith. This psalm portrays:

- The grandest conviction a person can have—God is mine and I am His. "Thou art my God; early will I seek thee" (v. 1).
- The grandest longing of body and soul—to thirst and long for God. "My flesh longeth for thee in a dry and thirsty land, where no water is" (v. 1).
- The grandest vision of life—the holy desire "to see [God's] power and [His] glory" (v. 2).
- The grandest song of praise—"Thy lovingkindness is better than life, my lips shall praise thee" (v. 3).
- The grandest satisfaction of the soul—the memory of God's goodness. "My soul shall be satisfied as with marrow and fatness; and my mouth shall praise thee with joyful lips" (v. 5).
- The grandest nighttime comfort—remembering God in the night. "When I remember thee upon my bed, and meditate on thee in the night watches" (v. 6).
- The surest and safest protection—the knowledge of God's past deliverances assures me of future safety under the shadow of His wings. "Because thou hast been my help, therefore in the shadow of thy wings will I rejoice" (v. 7).
- The grandest pursuit—"My soul followeth hard after thee" (v. 8).
- The most unfailing support—God's right hand (His hand of favor) sustains, supports, draws, and holds me. "Thy right hand upholdeth me" (v. 8).

- The grandest victory—God is with the righteous and delivers him from all enemies, including enemies of doubt, depression, fear, anger, and hopelessness (v. 9–11).

QUESTIONS

1. After reading Psalm 63 several times, what does it mean to me? How does it supply what I need right now?
2. What character qualities of God do I find in this psalm? (See Appendix A on page 291.)

Study

And that ye study to be quiet, and to do your own business, and to work with your own hands, as we commanded you. 1 Thessalonians 4:11

"That you study" literally means, "that you be ambitious" to be quiet. Some people when dealing with tragedy must talk and talk to someone, to anyone. Talking seems to release some of their pain. Others withdraw, not wanting to talk to anyone. They cry their tears and sob out their questions alone.

This imperative, "study to be quiet," is not necessarily about talking or not talking. It tells us not to be restless, uneasy, flighty, or fretful. It tells us to be restful, sedate, serene, calm, and peaceful. Finding that restful, calm spirit is difficult in this wild world of rush and grab, pause and go. Keeping a quiet heart is even more difficult when dealing with grief, pain, or disappointment, but it is possible.

If Jesus were to repeat this verse to one walking through a difficult valley, what might He mean? Maybe He would say:

> Be ambitious, my child—put forth effort to be still, to trust my love, to lean on my arm, to believe calmly in my plan. Tend to your business; go on with life. Though dark clouds of confusion surround you, in time they will give way to the sunshine of hope.
>
> Work with your own hands, though you feel exhausted and unmotivated. I will strengthen you as you put one foot before the other, as you do one duty and then the next. Do not operate on your emotions; act on your will. Rest often. Keep on keeping on.
>
> Resolve to be ambitious for this moment and I will give you strength for the next moment. In this study to be quiet, you will find rest, calmness, and peace.
>
> Your ever-present Help,
> Jesus

Grief is not quiet, calm, steady, or ambitious. It takes great effort to move from one moment to the next, from one duty to the next, from one trust to the next. Study! I must study the character of God and depend on His help. I must study the promises of God and believe them. I must study the quietness of God and rest in it.

Stillness, peacefulness, serenity, and trust require a definite ambition—study to attain. It is possible to be surrounded by that quietness! The Lord has brought me to that place again and again when I focus my mind on Him rather than on my situation.

As the wounds heal, those times of rest become longer. This is a growing process, and I must keep studying, studying to be God's restful servant.

QUESTIONS

1. Many people after a great loss, trial, or reverse in life become immobile like "a bump on a log." Grief has a way of removing all motivation and passion for living. What do I do when I do not feel like doing anything?
2. What is the difference between being unmotivated and being restful?
3. What effort must I put forth toward calmness and quietness? Or is that condition simply a gift from God?

Wait

Wait on the LORD: be of good courage, and he shall strengthen thine heart: wait, I say, on the LORD. Psalm 27:14

The Bible word *wait* has a number of meanings—expect, expect eagerly, await, wait with patience and confidence, continue steadfastly, abide.

Why is it that some of us find it so difficult to wait? We want action now! We want answers now! We want help and relief now!

Lord, calm my hasty, harried, hassled heart. My anxious spirit is at odds with your peaceful, composed, quiet Spirit. Lord, teach my heart to wait.

By God's grace and mercy I will:

- Wait at His door with patience and prayer.
- Wait at His heart with hope.
- Wait at His right hand with confidence.
- Wait at His feet with humility.
- Wait at His window where blessings are falling.
- Wait at His table with service.

When I learn to wait, I discover courage. Courage is cheer, confidence, and boldness. When I have courage, God will strengthen my heart. A strong heart makes a strong person. To live in this world of sin, sorrow, and pain, I need a strong heart. To live in this world of blessings, joys, and abundance, I need a strong heart. To face disappointments and turmoil, I need a strong heart. To face the valley of death, I need a strong heart.

When God tells me to wait, He speaks for a good reason. In waiting I find strength. Strength is the power to go on when moving forward seems impossible. Strength is seeing the ray of light in the dark valley and following it. Strength is remembering that I am never alone, even when I feel very much that way. Strength is accepting His disciplines as treasures and gifts of His love.

God took my heart and squeezed
Until I thought it would explode;
Then He whispered, "When I have tried you,
You shall come forth as gold."

—author unknown

QUESTIONS

1. How am I waiting on the Lord? In what frame of mind do I wait?
2. Have I experienced any blessings in waiting? What are they?
3. What am I finding it difficult to wait on?

Dealing with Depression

I will say unto God my rock, Why hast thou forgotten me? why go I mourning because of the oppression of the enemy? Psalm 42:9

What caused the writer's state of despair, depression, and loss of hope? Could God, who forgets nothing and no one, have forgotten His own child? Could He have forgotten to be merciful and gracious, longsuffering, and abundant in goodness? No! Has He closed up His mercies in His hand? No! Only a weak, faithless, sick, or guilty heart could suggest such a thought.

Often mental depression and spiritual darkness come because of physical weakness, hormonal imbalances, lack of sleep, or disease. Guilt, shame, and self-pity can also lead to depression. Besides working on the physical causes, we must spiritually fight and resist the wiles of Satan and self, which try to control the mind.

At the time of this writing, I am dealing with multiple griefs and also a genetic chemical imbalance. Besides dealing with those two stressors, I often struggle with negative thought patterns that lead into the black hole of depression. To break my negative thought patterns, I sometimes force myself to write a list of my blessings. Other times I do a word study of verses concerning God's mercy, forgiveness, faith, or a similar topic. When I write out the verses and a short commentary on them, I often find my depression lifting and my thought pattern changing.

Depression is a common aftereffect of grief. Some struggle with depression for months, and some for years, depending on a multitude of factors. No one likes to admit to having depression, but it is a most important admission in order to deal with it. I often remind myself that this, too, will pass!

God is always faithful in lifting me from despair; but I must do my part in resisting Satan, who loves to keep God's children depressed.

Depression has many faces, many causes, and varied depths of intensity. What helps one does not work for all; but God's love, His empathy, and His strength are there for everyone to utilize. I can choose to withdraw into the black hole or to reach out for help.

QUESTIONS

1. Is it correct to say a Christian never gets depressed?

2. What causes me to become depressed?
3. How do I fight my depression?
4. Read 1 Kings 21:2–4 and 1 Kings 19:1–6. What is the difference between Ahab's and Elijah's mindset? What was different about the cause of depression for each of them?
5. How did God care for Elijah in his depression?

The Stink

My wounds stink and are corrupt because of my foolishness. I am troubled; I am bowed down greatly; I go mourning all the day long. Psalm 38:5–6

I recognized the smell the moment I walked into the garage. Oh, no, not another dead mouse! I did not even want to look for it. How I hated the dead, stinking things!

I decided to ignore it. Perhaps sometime when my grandson came over he would find it and take it out. He did not seem to mind taking out dead mice.

Days went by. Every time I went to the garage, the horrible smell assaulted me. I determined I was not going to look for that stinking thing. Weeks went by. I always forgot to ask my grandson to find it when he came. The smell was so offensive to the nostrils that I kept the garage door open partway to let some of the stench dissipate into the clean air.

Finally, one day I had to go to the garage to get a bag of fertilizer. I opened the cabinet door and pulled out the bag. To my horror, out fell the decaying, dead mouse! Now I would have to take care of it.

What a lesson that dead, stinking mouse taught me! How often have I tried stuffing my pain and grief away so no one could see it? How often have I thought I would just ignore it, or pretend it was not there? I did not want to bring my grief out and look it in the face. Many times the reality of my losses just seemed too great to examine, too immense to deal with. Yet I could not ignore the stinking pain; I could not get away from the stench.

Then the God of tender mercy would nonchalantly drop a "dead mouse" at my feet and I would have to take care of it. Oh, the pain, the throbbing heart, the awful stink! Yet, oh, the blessing of peace and the comfort of His love that came when I submitted my pain to Him.

It is all right to cry. The hurt is necessary. Get on your knees, dig into my Word and find the oil of healing for your wounds. That is the way to take care of the stink, my child!

How many more dead mice will I have to deal with, Lord?

Let's not count them. Let's just deal with them as they appear. Do not wait for someone else to help you with your grief. You and I will deal with it together.

Putting off an easy thing makes it hard,
and putting off a hard one makes it impossible.[8]
—George Horace Lorimer

QUESTIONS

1. Have I tried stuffing my feelings? What have the results been?
2. Is there something I am putting off that really needs my attention?
3. How is God helping me to deal with my "dead mice"?
4. Procrastination is never advantageous, for I am either stealing time from someone else or myself. What lessons has procrastination taught me?

Never Alone

The LORD hear thee in the day of trouble; the name of the God of Jacob defend thee; send thee help from the sanctuary, and strengthen thee out of Zion. Psalm 20:1-2

The two-lane highway on my side of the road has suddenly narrowed to one lane. I find myself creeping through the traffic, feeling alone. I need to make decisions:

- Which way shall I go?
- Do I need fuel before the next city?
- Is there a detour that would make this easier?
- Why is traveling alone so confusing?

Everyone is traveling at a normal pace while I snail my way along. *Why, Lord, am I called to go this way alone? Why do I have to make these difficult decisions? Can you give me some answers, Lord?*

My child, you are never alone! I am with you always. Trust my judgment, lean on my arm, wait for my direction, and I will escort you in the way you should go. You need to keep yourself fueled constantly from my Word or you will not be ready for the next challenge, navigating the next big city. When I place your feet on a path, there is no safe detour. Move ahead slowly—with patience. Give yourself time and space to adjust to a different normal. Time and space help calm the confusion. Never compare your pace with others. They have their way to travel, but I have chosen a different path for you. I am your Pilot, Conductor, Guide, Leader, and Escort. Remember, I am also your Good Shepherd. Is that not enough?

When I feel alone and weary on the road I am traveling, I do well to pray as one evangelist prayed: "O God, keep my nerves from becoming tattered from the little conventionalities of our society, that they may be as strong as iron for the big issues of life. Keep me from becoming footsore in a mad race that leads almost nowhere, that I may have the readiness to take the steps that really count. In Christ's name, Amen."

Lord, help me to remember I must work my way through the valleys and up the mountains one step at a time. There are no elevators to my heavenly goal nor detours around my pain. I cannot twist my heart to adjust to the conventionalities of those who know no grief. I may not meet their expectations of how I ought to grieve. Help me to make it through this valley in a way that brings glory to your name.

How many times discouraged, we sink beside the way;
About us all is darkness, we hardly dare to pray.
Then thro' the mists and shadows, the sweetest voice e'er known
Says, "Child, am I not with thee, never to leave thee alone?"

No, never alone,
No, never alone;
He promised never to leave me,
Never to leave me alone.[9]

—Eben E. Rexford

QUESTIONS

1. What decisions do I need to make right now?
2. What causes me to feel alone?
3. In what ways do I try to conform to the opinions and judgments of others?
4. Do I often look for escape routes, or do I move courageously ahead in a time of distress or hardship?
5. How can I save my strength for the big issues of life?

Is Sin a Piece of the Puzzle?

Have mercy upon me, O God, according to thy lovingkindness: according unto the multitude of thy tender mercies blot out my transgressions. Psalm 51:1

David wrote this psalm from a broken and contrite heart. If the Bible remained silent about his sin of adultery and murder, we would greatly wonder what was wrong with David when he wrote this psalm. In the Bible, God always depicts the fallen state of man in honesty and straightforwardness. I must do the same with my life. A piece of the puzzle will always be missing, and the pain and turbulence will never be solved if I cover sin in my life.

David knew he was guilty of great sin, and he honestly pled for God's forgiveness. God's mercy and pity were David's only hope. How often is this our condition?

"My sin is ever before me" (Psalm 51:3). I bear my sin in my mind, I carry it in my body, I cannot forget it in my soul. The deeper my realization of sin, the greater my contrition will be.

David's faith in and love for God gave him hope in God's forgiveness. He cried out for mercy in sincerity and truth. He knew he did not deserve God's favor, but he trusted in God's love and mercy.

Dealing with grief can be much like dealing with sin in our lives. I often cry out to God from my grief-broken heart. I often seek His mercy in my sorrow. I seek relief from my pain, answers for my questions and help for my emotions. But do I come with a contrite heart seeking forgiveness for my sins? Do I come to Christ thinking He surely owes me consolation for my confusion and deliverance from my distress? Do my thought patterns and prayers imply He is the cause of all my pain and grief? After all, He took away my loved one!

I would never verbally blame God, yet at times my way of thinking, praying, and dealing with my grief treats Him as if He were guilty. God will not stand guilty before His creatures of dust! *Restore my mind, Lord. Redirect my thoughts and give me understanding and wisdom to know you are sovereign and righteous—your rightful self.*

All death is the result of sin. If man had not sinned in the Garden of Eden and passed on the sinful nature to all mankind, disease, sin, and death would not exist. Sin produces disease and death. Christ's death and resurrection bring regeneration and restoration. Because of God's loving-kindness, there is hope and heaven.

QUESTIONS

1. Are there any missing pieces in the puzzle of my present pain? Do I have any sin that is making this experience more difficult?
2. Have I always been honest with my family, with God, and with myself?
3. Have my prayers, my questions, and my seeking relief cast blame on Christ in any way?
4. Is there anything I can do to make God owe me something? Read Luke 17:7–10.

Don't Refuse Correction

O LORD, are not thine eyes upon the truth? thou hast stricken them, but they have not grieved; thou hast consumed them, but they have refused to receive correction: they have made their faces harder than a rock; they have refused to return. Jeremiah 5:3

What a tragedy! God spoke to His people in many ways, but they refused to listen. They rejected His commands. They chose to go their own way. He could not even get their attention.

What a grief it must be to the heart of God when He sends me His corrections and afflictions and I do not become better from them! What pain it must cause Him when I fail to learn what He is trying to teach me! Am I willing to go before God and say as Job did in Job 10:2, "Shew me wherefore thou contendest with me"? Am I open to what God is saying to me?

Even Job, whom Scripture calls "a perfect and an upright man," had something more to learn about God's sovereign power (Job 1:1). Job's testimony after his encounter with God was, "I have heard of thee by the hearing of the ear: but now mine eye seeth thee. Wherefore I abhor myself, and repent in dust and ashes" (Job 42:5–6). Job's losses, trials, and heartache taught him more about God and himself than he could have learned in a lifetime of ease.

Never doubt it—God knows how to get His point across! Will I learn the hard way like Israel did, or will I learn the gentler way by submission to God? Every bump in life's road, every difficult hill, and every patch of briers are a part of God's plan in perfecting His treasure in me. Keep me, Lord, from seeking a detour.

O Lord, you have stricken me! I beg for your blessing through this experience. May I learn what you are endeavoring to teach me that I might attain "the prize of the high calling of God in Christ Jesus" (Philippians 3:14).

God never ploughs in the soul of man
Without intention, purpose, and plan.

So whenever you feel the plough's sharp blade
Let not your heart be sorely afraid.

For, like the farmer, God chooses a field
From which He expects an excellent yield—

So rejoice though your heart is broken in two.
God seeks to bring forth a rich harvest in you.

—author unknown

The very fire that blackens my horizon warms my soul.
The darkness that oppresses my mind sharpens my vision.
The flood that overwhelms my heart quenches my thirst.
The thorns that penetrate my flesh strengthen my spirit.
The grave that buries my desires deepens my devotion.

—James Means

QUESTIONS

1. Have I disappointed God by not listening to Him?
2. What were some facts Job did not know about his terrible trial, facts that might have changed his whole outlook? Why did God hide those facts from him?
3. Might there be some facts I do not know about my painful situation?
4. What should I do about what I do not know?
5. In what ways have I refused correction?

My Glory or God's?

Whether therefore ye eat, or drink, or whatsoever ye do, do all to the glory of God. 1 Corinthians 10:31

No halo, Lord, but humility.
No glory, Lord, but in your cross.
Never holy and good in name alone;
Dependent and patient in gain or in loss.

No halo, Lord, but always faithful.
Keep my heart in your gracious hand.
Whatever I am is for your glory,
My life through sunshine and darkness—you have planned.

How often do I wish to be a wonderful woman of prayer, yet fail to reserve much time to meet with God? Sometimes I am like the woman who told the minister, "I would give everything in the world to be able to quote Scripture like you do."

The minister replied, "That is exactly what it takes." The woman walked sadly away.

How much time do I squander looking for wonders and miraculous revelations of God while failing to see His love and mercy in the everyday events of my life? Do I often miss the minute miracles of daily living while waiting and longing for the spectacular?

How much of the time do I live for my own glory? Do I feel that my suffering or calling places me in a higher position than that of my fellow Christians? Do I feel God is making a showpiece out of my piety? When humility is gone, pride has arrived, and the show glorifies me and not God. High aspirations for my spiritual life are only as good as the object of the aspirations. Do I aim to promote God or myself?

O God, help me to remember my calling is not to be in the spotlight of man's approval, nor to be well esteemed, nor to invoke pity from others. My calling is to live humbly every day to glorify your name in the common, daily duties of life. Help me, Lord, to keep my focus on your goal for me.

Let me be a desert spring—
No mirage on vision pressed—
But relief for thirsting pain
Bright oasis giving rest.

Christ the Water: His the flow
Filling every thirsty cup;
I the reservoir of clay
Hollowed deep to lift Him up!

—Mary Welch

QUESTIONS

1. What are my spiritual aspirations?
2. What is my most important goal in life?
3. Has this present tribulation caused me to lose sight of my goal, sharpened my view of it, or changed it?
4. Do I struggle with self-worth or pride?

Confusion—
What to Do with It?

If I be wicked, woe unto me; and if I be righteous, yet will I not lift up my head. I am full of confusion; therefore see thou mine affliction. Job 10:15

Was Job wondering whether he was being punished because of his sin or being tried to perfect his righteousness? How often I have wondered the same thing!

Someone said, "An honest look at life will bring confusion." Indeed, life is full of perplexities and injustice. Without an eternal perspective on these things, losses can bring us to a growing mountain of confusion, a valley of disappointments, and a river of pain and tears.

Looking back, I wonder if my father's absence during my childhood was God's way of preparing me for future losses. Was my being one of a kind, the only Mennonite girl in a school of over a thousand students, developing my backbone to stand alone later in life? Were my disappointments and confusion God's way to create a hunger for Him and a dependent trust in His care? Only God knows and understands the circumstances for which He was preparing me. It has been, and is, a long, painful road of learning.

When we honestly face our confusion, it causes us to thirst for God. My confusion and disappointment concerning my father leaving us for weeks, months, and one time for a year with no knowledge of his whereabouts, mostly served to make me distrustful and suspicious of men. I accepted what Larry Crabb describes as the common "Christian" strategy for ending confusion—"Deny the reality of disturbing questions behind renewed commitment to God."[10] Crabb continues, "Such a strategy produces rigid dogmatism which saps our faith of vitality."[11] How true! I worked hard at being the model student, the obedient child, the good daughter. I was building my image in hope of preserving our family image—pretending there were relationships that really did not exist.

Larry Crabb also says, "No amount of responsibility taking will ever relieve the thirst for relationship. Only heaven offers complete satisfaction. Until then, a disturbing sense of incompleteness will continue to blemish the most responsible and most blessed life. We can deny it, we can cover it over with busyness and pleasures, but we cannot get rid of it."[12]

When those longed-for human relationships never develop, or bring continual disappointment, I must turn to God and seek to renew and enhance my relationship with Him.

Heaven is God's best cure for confusion and disappointments.

QUESTIONS

1. What human relationships have been or are disappointing to me?
2. How have I disappointed someone I love?
3. What is presently confusing me?
4. How is my confusion creating a thirst for God?

Forgiveness

For if ye forgive men their trespasses, your heavenly Father will also forgive you: but if ye forgive not men their trespasses, neither will your Father forgive your trespasses. Matthew 6:14–15

A heart of resentment, a jealous attitude, or a physical sickness often develops when there is an unforgiving spirit. Buried bitter feelings frequently produce physical illness. A sick mind and soul often result in a sick body. If my mind is in a state of dis-ease, my body will react with disease.

In addition to causing serious physical consequences, a refusal to forgive cuts us off from God's forgiveness, according to the verses above. Not only is forgiveness a gift I extend to others, but it is also a gift I give myself—a gift of renewed health of body, soul, and spirit. Only God can settle the debt that harasses my mind, the debt I think I owe or the debt I think someone owes me. Bitterness and guilt are hard taskmasters. I become a slave to the person I refuse to forgive. I must give my hurt to God, and He will give me healing. I must choose to forgive.

Sometimes I fear telling God all my inner turmoil and bad feelings. This is a very unreasonable fear, since God already knows my thoughts before I think them. "Thou knowest my downsitting and mine uprising, thou understandest my thought afar off" (Psalm 139:2). Perhaps it is too humbling to admit that my bitterness or my thoughts have dumped me into such a low ditch. I will never find relief and healing until I am willing to open the "can of worms" and present them before God one by horrible one. Only God can offer forgiveness and healing, and He can do so only when I choose to change my attitude toward the object of my anger, bitterness, or jealousy.

Bernard of Clairvaux said, "Nothing can work me damage except myself. The harm that I sustain I carry about with me, and am never a real sufferer but by my own fault."[13]

A person facing grief will find that statement difficult to understand or believe until he moves further through the grief process and seeks healing. A time comes when each griever will come to understand the healing or damaging effects of his attitude toward his grief.

QUESTIONS

1. Is my current trial causing physical problems? Do I have anger, bitterness, guilt or jealousy hidden in my heart?
2. The following questions help me determine whether or not I have truly forgiven:
    a. Do I no longer avoid the person? Am I comfortable around the person?
    b. Do I feel love, tenderness, and understanding toward that person?
    c. Do I speak kindly about that person to others?
    d. Can I think about the person without rehearsing the details of his offense in my mind?
    e. Can I look the person in the eyes with friendly feelings in my heart?
    f. Can I pray for the blessings of God on that person?

The Power of Attitude

But if ye have bitter envying and strife in your hearts, glory not, and lie not against the truth. This wisdom descendeth not from above, but is earthly, sensual, devilish. For where envying and strife is, there is confusion and every evil work. But the wisdom that is from above is first pure, then peaceable, gentle, and easy to be intreated, full of mercy and good fruits, without partiality, and without hypocrisy. And the fruit of righteousness is sown in peace of them that make peace. James 3:14–18

If I think bitterness and anger, I will be consumed by bitterness and anger. If I think love and forgiveness, I will be permeated with love and forgiveness. I am free to choose how I respond to life and its absurdities. Our thoughts shape who we are, as Proverbs 23:7 says: "For as he thinketh in his heart, so is he."

Victor Frankl suffered torture and unmentionable indignities while imprisoned in the death camps of World War II in Germany. His parents, his brother, and his wife all died in the camps or the gas ovens. His sister was the only survivor from his immediate family. What grief he must have known!

Everything was taken away from Victor, including his clothes. Yet, his testimony was, "Everything can be taken from a man but one thing: the last of human freedoms—to choose one's attitude in any given set of circumstances."[14] This was the one freedom his Nazi captors could not take away. They could control his entire environment and do what they wanted with his body. But they could not destroy his inner identity. He still had the power within himself to determine how his outer circumstances and the Nazis' treatment of him were going to affect his inner self. He could not choose the circumstances in which he found himself, but he could choose the attitude with which he would respond.

I must never forget my power to choose a response. Eve used that same God-given power to sin in the garden of Eden. She chose to respond wrongly to Satan.

If God had not given me the power of choice, I would be nothing more than a puppet, a marionette who jerks at the whim of the puppeteer pulling the strings. The power to choose is a privilege that can keep me free and alive, or a hindrance that can imprison and kill me. As long as I use my God-given power to respond rightly, I will never become a victim of bitterness, hatred, or anger.

My journey through the dark valley presents many challenges to choose my attitude toward what happens. I will remember that God does all things for my good. That fact can be a real attitude adjustor for me, especially when I am hurting and confused about what He is doing in my life.

> No man is free who is not master of his thoughts.
>
> —author unknown

QUESTIONS

1. How much power do thoughts have over the body?
2. What enabled Victor Frankl to remain a sane, loving individual?
3. Why did God give me the power of choice?
4. What are some attitude choices I need to make concerning my current trial?

Tears

When Jesus therefore saw her weeping, and the Jews also weeping which came with her, he groaned in the spirit, and was troubled, and said, Where have ye laid him? They said unto him, Lord, come and see. Jesus wept. John 11:33-35

Jesus wept tears of bereavement at the grave of Lazarus. "Then said the Jews, Behold how he loved him!" (John 11:36). Even though Jesus knew He would bring Lazarus back to life, He wept, acknowledging the pain of loss because of His love for His friend.

For me, tears of bereavement relieve the mind as well as the heart. These tears show sympathy; they express the heart's innermost feelings of pain, distress, and helplessness. They show honor and love for the departed one. Moreover, these tears are the wordless prayers to God for help, comfort, and hope. As Queen Elizabeth II said, "Grief is the price we pay for love."

Jesus wept tears of concern over Jerusalem. "O Jerusalem, Jerusalem, which killest the prophets, and stonest them that are sent unto thee; how often would I have gathered thy children together, as a hen doth gather her brood under her wings, and ye would not!" (Luke 13:34). "And when he was come near, he beheld the city, and wept over it" (Luke 19:41). He deeply felt His chosen people's rejection of and unresponsiveness to His redeeming love.

For me, tears of concern represent frustration and disappointment. They are tears of anxiety and sometimes tears of despair. My tears of concern are often for my situation and myself. When will my situation change? Will life ever get better, or will bad things continue to happen? When will I learn that God's dealings are not bad? Am I learning what God wants me to learn?

As I continue to heal, I find myself shedding tears of concern for others, tears of love and compassion, tears of reaching out and touching the bleeding hearts of others. I must allow God to reach in and heal my pain so that I am more fully able to minister to the needs of others.

Jesus wept tears of mental anguish in the Garden of Gethsemane. "Then saith he unto them, My soul is exceeding sorrowful, even unto death: tarry ye here, and watch with me. And he went a little further, and fell on his face, and prayed, saying, O my Father, if it be possible, let this cup pass from me: nevertheless not as I will, but as thou wilt" (Matthew 26:38–39).

The weight of the sins of mankind was on the heart and mind of Jesus. How painful that weight of sin must have been on the pure, holy, uncontaminated, righteous, devout life of our Savior! We cannot imagine the immensity of the heaviness.

For me, tears of mental anguish flow at times when I am trying to understand the "hard hand of God" in my life. These tears come when I find obedience difficult and trust almost impossible. These tears must wash away my stubbornness and flood my heart with acquiescence to my Father's will. I must learn to say as Jesus said: "Not my will, but thine, be done" (Luke 22:42).

Jesus' tears of anguish melded His will into His Father's will.

QUESTIONS

1. What do the tears of Jesus mean to me?
2. Tears come for different reasons. What are some occasions and reasons for my tears?
3. Are all tears good? Can tears be selfish or rebellious?

Coping or Casting?

I will be glad and rejoice in thy mercy: for thou hast considered my trouble; thou hast known my soul in adversities. Psalm 31:7

Some days you tame the tiger. And some days the tiger has you for lunch.
—Tug McGraw

Do you feel you have some pretty good coping skills? What are your coping skills: stuffing, mind control, people control, blaming, crying, praying, denying, dreaming? We each have different ways of coping with painful situations and trials. Some are helpful and good, while others are destructive and wrong.

I once thought I knew how to cope with some situations, but I have come to realize I cannot handle anything on my own. When life hands us one impossible problem after another, one grievous loss after another, we suddenly realize we have no inner resources except our faith in the goodness of God. When hardships exhaust all human wisdom, human reasoning, human knowledge, and human strength, we must reach out for God's sovereign wisdom, His incomprehensible knowledge, and His infinite strength, mercy, and love.

The word *cope* is not in God's vocabulary. It is not in the Bible. God does not want us to try to cope; He tells us to "cast."

- What do I do with my burdens? "Cast thy burden upon the LORD, and he shall sustain thee: he shall never suffer the righteous to be moved" (Psalm 55:22).
- What do I do with my wild imagination? "Casting down imaginations, and every high thing that exalteth itself against the knowledge of God, and bringing into captivity every thought to the obedience of Christ" (2 Corinthians 10:5).
- What do I do with my troubles and cares? "Casting all your care upon him; for he careth for you" (1 Peter 5:7).
- What do I do with my failures and sins? "Behold, for peace I had great bitterness: but thou hast in love to my soul delivered it from the pit of corruption: for thou hast cast all my sins behind thy back" (Isaiah 38:17).

God's command to cast works much better than our trying to cope.

Cast yourself at Jesus' feet;
You will find love, joy, and peace complete.

It is God's knowledge of me,
His careful husbanding of the ground of my being,
His constant presence in the garden of my little life
that guarantees my joy.
—W. Phillip Keller

QUESTIONS

1. What are my most common coping skills?
2. Are any of my coping skills destructive?
3. Based on James 1:5, when I do not know how to handle a situation, what should I do?
4. Why do I so often find myself trying to cope with my problem rather than casting it on the Lord?

Grieving in Hope

But I would not have you to be ignorant, brethren, concerning them which are asleep, that ye sorrow not, even as others which have no hope. For if we believe that Jesus died and rose again, even so them also which sleep in Jesus will God bring with him. 1 Thessalonians 4:13–14

How differently we each deal with death and grief! I tend to seek relief from grief by spending time alone with God. Some people want company every night. Some want companionship, needing someone to eat with them, talk with them, and even sleep with them. Other people want to be alone.

Some people laugh and joke to release their emotions. Some find relief through tears. At times, most people who are grieving will find themselves uptight, with taut nerves. Some have quick tempers. Others live in a world detached from everything and everyone around them.

Some enjoy talking endlessly about the deceased; some do not want to hear the deceased's name mentioned. Some immerse themselves in memories and photos; others cannot tolerate the sight of photos.

Some quickly get rid of all the belongings of the deceased. Some will not go into the bedroom where their loved one passed away. Some wash their loved one's clothes each week just as they did while he/she lived. Some pack away all the belongings of the deceased, while some just keep a special object or piece of clothing.

Yes, we all deal with grief differently. Who does it right? Who does it wrong? Who am I to say? I am just another human who deals with grief the way I do because of who I am.

God tells us in James 1:2 to "count it all joy when ye fall into divers temptations" (testings, trials). His will is for us to grieve, not selfishly or defiantly, but meekly with a surrendered spirit. When it comes to how we process our grief, however, He does not insist that we all grieve in one prescribed way. He does give us a guideline to remember: "Sorrow not, even as others which have no hope" (1 Thessalonians 4:13).

How I grieve can immobilize me or nudge me forward. It certainly affects the way I feel about the future and about my own time of leaving this earth. There is hope now and ahead!

At End

At end of view, at end of life,
At end of hope, at end of strife,

At end of all we cling to so,
The sun is setting—must we go?

At dawn of view, at dawn of life,
At dawn of peace there is no strife,

At dawn of all we long for so,
The sun is rising—let us go.

—Louise Chandler Moulton

QUESTIONS

1. How do I deal with grief, pain, or stress?
2. Am I finding God's grace sufficient during this troubled time?
3. In what ways has God shown me mercy?
4. Am I living more in the past, or are my steps moving forward?

Maintenance

I know that the LORD will maintain the cause of the afflicted, and the right of the poor. Psalm 140:12

Some days we get up in the morning feeling as if we have nothing to go on—no power, no strength, no motivation to keep us going through the day. Many mornings I have cried out to God, *O Lord, maintain me! Supply what I need to make it through this day.*

The verse from Psalm 140 assures me that "the LORD will maintain the cause of the afflicted." Another verse in 1 Kings 8:45 offers this prayer: "Then hear thou in heaven their prayer and their supplication, and maintain their cause." In addition, a promise is given in Psalm 16:5: "The LORD is the portion of mine inheritance and of my cup: thou maintainest my lot." Jude 21 gives us this command: "Keep yourselves in the love of God, looking for the mercy of our Lord Jesus Christ unto eternal life."

What is my part if I want God to maintain my lot? I must remain in His love, keeping Him as the center of my life.

A vehicle needs gas, oil, brake fluid, water, and good tires to maintain it and keep it running. Like a car, our relationship with God needs careful maintenance. The kind of maintenance we need varies according to our personalities. For me, a lot of my maintenance involves controlling my thoughts and taking time to be still and listen to God.

When someone I love is dealing with cancer or any other life-threatening situation, it is too easy to let my imaginations and emotions run wild. When I do this, I become useless to myself and to others. *Lord, I need a relaxed, trusting, peaceful, positive spirit!*

I can control my anxious thoughts by keeping God and His power in focus, remembering His love and many answers to my pleas, and praising Him for His faithfulness in filling me with strength in times of weakness. *Lord, help me maintain a heart of gratitude.*

"If thou prepare thine heart, and stretch out thine hands toward him; if iniquity be in thine hand, put it far away, and let not wickedness dwell in thy tabernacles. For then shalt thou lift up thy face without spot; yea, thou shalt be stedfast, and shalt not fear" (Job 11:13–15).

God, keep my heart steadfastly anchored in your sure promises and your love for me. I want to be steadfast like a post that is concreted in the fencerow or an anchor that is heavy enough to hold the ship in the storm.

"For we are made partakers of Christ, if we hold the beginning of our confidence steadfast unto the end" (Hebrews 3:14).

How does the Lord maintain me? The ways are too numerous to list! He gives me miraculous emotional and physical strength when I'm called to serve others. He catches my tears and puts them in His bottle, anointing me with healing. He puts me to sleep many times. He calms my troubled heart and fills me with peace. He sends someone who needs help and He sends someone to help me. He wakes me with a song. Yes, He maintains my cause!

QUESTIONS

1. In what ways do I need the Lord to maintain me?
2. What is my part in staying maintained?
3. How has God maintained me in the past week?
4. I need to face my feelings and talk to God about them. What emotions am I dealing with?
5. What attitudes might I have that would prevent God from maintaining my heart?

Soul Rest

Return unto thy rest, O my soul; for the LORD hath dealt bountifully with thee. Psalm 116:7

God is the promised rest for my soul. This rest is the rightful possession of the soul. God did not create the soul to be in a perpetual state of worry, anxiety, and distress, such as many people experience.

When I go through difficult and painful experiences, it is too easy to focus on my problems, which pushes my soul into distress. Or, I may lose my rest by neglecting to seek God or submit to His will. Disobedience and unbelief remove rest from my soul.

There is a reason this verse says, "Return to your rest." What I have left, what I have lost, I must return to. It is my duty to regain, reclaim, and get back the rest that God gave me and has promised me.

When I am at rest, my heart is at peace, my mind is tranquil, and my soul is relaxed in trusting confidence. When I am not at rest, I experience confusion, turmoil, doubt, and fear.

Life is the proving ground of my rest. My rest-testing comes in so many forms; disappointments, losses, failures, weaknesses (physical and spiritual), worldly success, activities, busyness, friends, and enemies all have the potential of testing my rest.

I have so often perturbed my rest by busyness. I seek to boost my self-esteem and gain the approval of others by keeping busy, by saying yes and jumping at everyone's demand. Someone once said, "*No* is one of the hardest words in the English language to learn." I can never learn the reality of God's rest until I learn to say no.

For others, "no" and inactivity are the easy way. William Cowper said, "Absence of occupation is not rest; a mind quite vacant is a mind distressed."[15]

Lord, give me balance! Keep me out of the ditch of catering to the demands of others and out of the opposite ditch of doing only what pleases me. Keep me out of the ditch of laziness and out of the contrasting ditch of overwork. In the balance of your will I can find rest. When I am tried by fire, the way I act or react will prove whether or not my soul is at rest. O Lord, sometimes it takes so little to disturb my rest. How often I need to return to my rest! How often I must return to you in penitence and trust. How often I need to remind myself of your bountiful care for me. You love me, forgive me, and restore me bountifully.

QUESTIONS

1. Do I feel at rest or am I plagued by anxiety and distress?
2. What do I do to regain a restful spirit?
3. Was there a time when I had a hard time saying no? What did that do for my spirit? Am I still that way? If not, what caused me to change?

Laugh

He healeth the broken in heart, and bindeth up their wounds. Psalm 147:3

Bodily pain directly affects the spirit, and pain in the spirit affects the body. With each dark valley and each loss, I have faced a new set of ailments in my body. Negative emotions threaten to rule and ruin my body.

With each painful blow, I have cried out to God, the tender, compassionate Healer—the One who offers tender words, healing touch, and true empathy. Only He can heal my broken heart; only He knows and understands all my bodily weaknesses. He knows my struggles to be strong, and how hard I try to keep up with the pace of life around me.

How often He reminds me I do not need to be strong! I do not need to keep up. How often He tells me to just rest in His arms! He supplies strength when I really need it and rest when it really does not matter if I don't keep up.

How important is it that I take my broken heart and deep wounds to the Lord? Very important! Many suffer dire results because they do not take their pain to the Lord. The emotional pain caused by divorce is often as traumatic on the body and emotions as the death of a loved one. In his book, *Deadly Emotions*, Don Colbert, M. D., tells of a nurse who reported, "I know of at least two dozen people who developed very serious diseases two to five years after their divorces. At least nine of those people have died."[16] Disease is not strictly physical; often it is emotional. In fact, Colbert goes on to say that the largest percentage of sickness he sees is brought about by the emotions: "The body cannot differentiate between stress that physical factors cause and stress that emotional factors cause. Stress is stress."[17]

I find myself battling with Satan's lie, "You'll never laugh again." I know life will never be the same again, but I must give myself the privilege of smiling and laughing again. Proverbs 15:13 says, "A merry heart maketh a cheerful countenance: but by sorrow of the heart the spirit is broken." God never allows our heart to be broken or our spirit wounded so that we will not heal again, so that we will never be happy again.

Dr. William Fry, Jr. says that laughter is as beneficial to health as exercise: "Laughter ventilates the lungs and leaves the muscles, nerves, and heart warm and relaxed."[18] Laughter has also proved to decrease cortisol—a stress hormone—and adrenaline, while increasing the feel-good hormone endorphin and the growth or youth hormone. So laughter is healing to the body, soul, and spirit. The Great Physician has the remedy for the broken heart and the wounded spirit.

> Smiles are created in you—it's up to you to choose to express them!
>
> —author unknown

QUESTIONS

1. In what ways has my body been affected by trauma?
2. Have I ever become sick because of my emotions?
3. Do I find it easy or difficult to laugh?
4. What do smiling and laughing do for me?

Recovery

And they that shall be of thee shall build the old waste places: thou shalt raise up the foundations of many generations; and thou shalt be called, The repairer of the breach, The restorer of paths to dwell in. Isaiah 58:12

I had spent more than an hour working on the layout for a newsletter. I saved the document, and later when I tried to open it, I was shocked to read the message, "Corrupted file. Open and recover or convert your file." How could I do that?

I checked the help button and tried to follow the directions, but got the same despairing message. I had learned how to use a computer by trial and error, and I was still learning!

As I shut off the computer, I decided to forget my lost work and begin a new document. By the next day, my frustration had subsided so I could think clearly, and I decided to try one more time to open the document. This time directions came up on how to recover it. I read and followed the directions. There was an arrow right by the "Open" button and when I clicked on the arrow, a menu dropped down, and there was the "Recover" key! I clicked on it and hoped. It worked! There was my document with all my work!

My problem had taught me something new. After more than twenty-five years of working on the computer, why had I never noticed that arrow beside the "Open" button? Because I never needed it or I simply ignored it.

I have been astonished at the new things I learn when I have a problem on the computer. I have learned more new things through problems than by studying the manual. Often this is the hard way to learn, but it is the way it sticks the best for me.

The lessons I learn through my problems on the computer are analogous to my Christian life. Problems and trials have taught me more than a happy, comfortable life ever could have taught me. God's Word and His work in my life teach me new truths daily. I find new truths in a verse or passage I have read often. Sometimes God uses the same trial or a different one to teach me the same lesson over again. I forget so quickly.

If my computer work is parallel to my walk with God, I wonder why God didn't give me a recovery button. When circumstances shatter my hopes and dreams, I need a recovery button. When I am crushed with grief, I need a recovery button.

When Satan strangles me with despair, I need a recovery button. When Satan corrupts my life in a dozen ways, I need a recovery button. *Lord, where is my recovery button?*

My child, your recovery button is on your knees. Your recovery button is in my Word. Your recovery button is under that arrow—that dark cloud where you find faith. Your recovery button is in my listening ears, outstretched hands, and understanding heart. I am your recovery button.

Oh, yes, Lord. I have used those recovery buttons many times! Help me, Lord, to remember you are there, and I shall recover.

We often learn more from our problems than our successes.

Turn your face toward the sun and the shadows will fall behind you.
—Maori Proverb

QUESTIONS

1. From what do I need to recover?
2. Does my progress or lack of progress show my acceptance or lack of acceptance of God's will?
3. What do I use as my recovery button?

PART TWO
LEARNING TO TRUST

Progress

Until I learned to trust,
I did not learn to pray;
And I did not learn to fully trust
Till sorrows came my way.

Until I felt my weakness,
His strength I never knew;
Nor dreamed till I was stricken
That He would see me through.

Who deepest drinks of sorrow,
Drinks deepest, too, of grace.
God sends the storm so He Himself
Can be our hiding place;

His heart that seeks our highest good
Knows well when things annoy.
We would not long for heaven
If earth held only joy.

—author unknown

Fear

What time I am afraid, I will trust in thee. In God I will praise his word, in God I have put my trust; I will not fear what flesh can do unto me. Psalm 56:3–4

Do I know where to go when my heart quivers with fear? Have I made the commitment David made to trust in the Lord?

After my multiple losses, I must admit to having fears of losing other family members. When part of my family is going on a trip, I often have to seek God's help in dealing with fear. Age and life's circumstances have developed in me an incredible fear of water and fire—fears I never had when younger.

One experience made me aware of how controlling and powerful my fear was. My grandchildren went out to walk the coast in the dark. There was very little coastline because the tide was high. I could not understand why anyone would want to walk the coast, in the dark, at high tide. I kept my fear hidden from the rest of the family. Finally, I had to get away alone and cry out to God. My heart was pounding, my head was throbbing, my stomach was churning. I had to regain control of my emotions. After pleading and praying for God to take away my fear, after crying out for a greater trust in God, I finally began to calm down. Peace slowly crept into my heart. I would trust God. What other option was there? I thanked God for His control and calmly waited for the grandchildren's safe return.

After this incident, I read a story of a man who was terribly fearful of all kinds of things. One night he heard footsteps on the deck outside his bedroom window. Instead of jumping up, getting a light, and looking to see what made the noise, he froze in bed. In a short time, he could hardly get his breath. He wakened his wife, who immediately called 911. His gray pallor and difficulty breathing told her he was having a heart attack. He survived his heart attack and came home to learn that the neighbors had gotten a big dog the day before his emergency. The sound that caused him such fear in the night was probably the big dog exploring his new neighborhood.

Nabal had a heart attack when he heard the fearful news that David had intended to kill him. "But it came to pass in the morning, when the wine was gone out of Nabal, and his wife had told him these things, that his heart died within him, and he became as a stone" (1 Samuel 25:37). Fear can paralyze, fear can enslave, fear can kill.

The man who fears suffering is already suffering from what he fears.
—Michel de Montaigne

Fear Him, ye saints, and you will then have nothing else to fear.[19]
—Nahum Tate and Nicholas Brady

The assurance that God cannot possibly inflict wrong should free us from the slavery of fear.

QUESTIONS

1. What causes me to be fearful?
2. When I begin to panic because of fear, what do I do to help myself?
3. Do I have particular reasons for particular fears?
4. How does fear affect me physically?

When It Pleased God

But when it pleased God, who separated me from my mother's womb, and called me by his grace, to reveal his Son in me, that I might preach him among the heathen; immediately I conferred not with flesh and blood. Galatians 1:15–16

"When it pleased God." God has a plan! God has a timetable. God has a purpose He will accomplish when it pleases Him.

O Lord, forgive me for questioning your divine plan, but I'd really like to know—

When will it please you to awaken my son to his spiritual needs?

When will it please you to heal my daughter?

When will it please you to grant me a year of "normal" living?

When will it please you to heal my pain?

When will it please you to answer my endless prayers?

O God, my expectations wait on you to be fulfilled!

And God's reply is, ***Why do you limit me by your plan and your expectations? Give me some "elbow room." My thoughts are higher than your thoughts. My ways are higher than your ways. Give me room to work out my plan, in my way, when it pleases me.***

Yes, Lord, I plead your mercy and understanding. Fill my frail humanity with your spirit and your power. Give me the trust and anticipation that waits in faith and patience for your design, without my human input. Help me to give you more than "elbow room"!

When God is working the way He desires to work—in His time, on His plan—it is not the time for me to seek counsel, help, or understanding from humans. Paul said, "When it pleased God, . . . immediately I conferred not with flesh and blood." When it pleased God to call Paul and to reveal His Son in him, Paul went to Arabia in seclusion with God for three years of training. There he heard only God's voice and learned to live and work according to God's plan.

Conferring with other humans about my trials and pain, when God is calling me to commune with Him, often muddies the waters of affliction. Although there are stages of my valley journey when I need a human hand and heart to love me, lift me, and assist me, sometimes God wants me to come to Him alone and wait for His time.

QUESTIONS

1. What am I waiting for God's timetable to accomplish? What are some things I expect God to achieve in my life, or in the life of one I love?
2. Am I willing to wait for God's plan or am I pushing my plan? How am I waiting or pushing?
3. Do I really believe God has a purpose and plan for this pain, this delay, this trial?
4. Do I really believe that God can turn all my hard, painful troubles into something good and beneficial for me? What benefits or growth do I feel as a result of my current crisis?

In the Refining Pot

Therefore am I troubled at his presence: when I consider, I am afraid of him. For God maketh my heart soft, and the Almighty troubleth me. Job 23:15–16

Job had suffered severely. God had put him in the "refining pot" many times. Job was at the point of thinking, *How likely is it that God will act in the future other than how He has acted in the past? God does that which seems best to Him, and He does not change.*

Job's heart was tremulous—all courage was gone and he was prey to terror and wild imaginations. He expected nothing but more suffering.

In spite of his inner turmoil, Job had two facts right: God does what seems best to Him, and He does not change. However, in his deep sorrow and pain, Job had temporarily lost sight of the love, grace, mercy, and goodness of God. How often we do the same when we are severely tried!

When bad things happen, we fear that more will follow. The terror of "What's coming next?" can set the stage for a chain of painful events—real or imaginary. It takes great effort to stop the avalanche of terrified imaginations.

When I am in the refining pot, I need to immerse myself in studying the attributes of God. The better I know God, and the more time I spend with Him, the more comfort and hope I will experience. My relationship with Him will deepen.

God is incomprehensible
God is self-sufficient
God is infinite
God is omniscient
God is omnipotent
God is faithful
God is mercy
God is love
God is sovereign
God is self-existent
God is eternal
God is immutable
God is wisdom
God is omnipresent
God is just
God is grace
God is holy
God is triune

God knows my weakness, my distress, my fears, so He promises to go with me wherever I go. He promises to be my light, my love, and even my life. He knows better than I that I cannot live acceptably and successfully without His help and His direction.

"God is light, and in him is no darkness at all" (1 John 1:5).

GOD IS LIGHT . . .

When the day is overcast,
In the night wind's stormy blast.

GOD IS LIGHT . . .

When your thoughts are lone and bleak,
When your heart feels dim and weak, GOD IS LIGHT.

"God is love; and he that dwelleth in love dwelleth in God, and God in him" (1 John 4:16).

GOD IS LOVE . . .

When you feel forsaken by all,
When your dearest answered God's call.

GOD IS LOVE . . .

When you have failed over time,
And life's without reason or rhyme, GOD IS LOVE.

"Jesus saith unto him, I am the way, the truth, and the life" (John 14:6).

GOD IS LIFE . . .

When the cold grave holds the dead,
When your dreams are filled with dread.

GOD IS LIFE . . .

When earthly life is finished and done,
And when victories are all won, GOD IS ETERNAL LIFE!

QUESTIONS

1. What attributes of God do I depend on most during tribulation?
2. If I feel I am in God's refining pot, do I believe God is accomplishing something good in my life? What do I believe He is accomplishing?

God's Response to Discouragement

[Elijah] said, It is enough; now, O LORD, take away my life; for I am not better than my fathers. 1 Kings 19:4

Elijah was discouraged. Discouragement often comes after a great victory just as Elijah's did.

Elijah told God:	**God replied:**
I am tired and weary.	Sleep in peace.
I am not hungry.	Arise and eat. The journey is great.
Nobody cares.	I care.
This is more than I can handle.	I can do anything.
I am all alone—the only one left.	I have a backup of seven thousand.
It is enough! Let me die.	I have work for you to do.
I have been jealous for God, and it has done no good.	In a still, small voice, "I am with you."

- Discouragement distorts our vision and skews our perspective.
- Discouragement overlooks God's presence and care.
- Discouragement leaves us feeling hopeless and without purpose.
- Discouragement drains the body of strength and the heart of trust.
- Discouragement causes us to forget that this, too, will pass.
- Discouragement brings doubts, fears, and insecurity.
- Discouragement strains relationships.
- Discouragement opens the door for Satan.
- Discouragement closes the door to God's possibilities.

Let's remember who the master of discouragement is and let's pray continually to stay out of his snares. Each day God offers us a fresh opportunity to live in His grace and mercy. Let's listen to the voice of God for His response to our discouraged thoughts.

God, give me the grit, God give me the grace
To not drop out, but to run life's full race.
Lord, I am resolved to never resign,
With your grand help, I'll cross the finish line.

—author unknown

Never again:

Think of yourself as alone—for I am with you.
Think of yourself as defenseless—for I am your protector.
Think of yourself as inadequate—for I am your provider.
Think of yourself as useless—for I have a purpose for you.
Think of yourself as hopeless—for I am your future.
Think of yourself as unaccepted—for I love you very much.

—Jesus

QUESTIONS

1. What is causing me discouragement right now?
2. How does discouragement affect me? How do I act and react?
3. What was God's remedy for Elijah's discouragement?
4. What might be God's remedy for my discouragement?

Refreshing Springs

All my springs are in thee. Psalm 87:7

He sendeth the springs into the valleys, which run among the hills. Psalm 104:10

A spring is where I go for a refreshing drink.

A spring is where I go for a cooling splash after a hot, tiring day.

A spring is where I rinse the dust of the day from my dirty feet and hands.

Christ is the fountain of life and of all human good. My springs are in Him—He is my source of life, joy, and happiness. He alone is my source of refreshment when I feel faint from the battle of life. Only His love can cool and calm me after a torrent of tears. Only His forgiveness can wash the grime of unbelief, the dirt of self-will from my heart. After His refreshing cleansing, He alone can restore my hope and confidence in His care. He alone heals my heart so I can reach out and touch other hurting hearts with His refreshment.

Help me, Lord, to look for fountains of refreshment:

- *In worship, prayer, and praise.*
- *In all of creation's beauties.*
- *In simple joys of daily living.*
- *In what you have done for me in the past.*
- *In what you are doing for me presently.*
- *In what you are going to do for me in the future.*
- *In the trustworthiness of your character.*

One of the best ways to be refreshed is to concentrate on the positive elements in our lives while surrendering the negative things to God.

Lord, strengthen my awareness and appreciation for:

- *Good memories.*
- *The good years you gave me.*
- *Sharing and caring times.*
- *Family ties and friendships.*

- *My relationship with you.*
- *The certainty of your presence.*
- *The guarantee of your promises.*
- *The comfort of your love.*
- *The peace of your salvation.*
- *Countless daily blessings.*

Thank you, Lord, for the comfort and hope in the blessings you have given.

When all created streams are dried, His fullness is the same.

Not now, but in the coming years,
It may be in the better land,
We'll read the meaning of our tears,
And there sometime, we'll understand.

Then trust in God through all the days;
Fear not, for He doth hold thy hand;
Though dark thy way, still sing and praise,
Sometime, sometime, we'll understand.[20]

—Maxwell N. Cornelius

QUESTIONS

1. How has Jesus been like a spring of fresh water to me?
2. What things of the world have I tried without finding refreshment?
3. What in my spirit, emotions, or body feels dry and in need of refreshment?
4. What elements of God's character do I especially need right now?

Sweet in Adversity

If thou faint in the day of adversity, thy strength is small. Proverbs 24:10

Let me tell you the true story of Mr. Miller the cat. Mr. Miller was just a common, friendly, farm cat. He loved to curl up and sleep with the family dog. He ran and played with the other cats. He frolicked with the children.

One day, Mr. Miller was sleeping on the drive when a young man jumped into a truck and roared out the lane. Poor Mr. Miller suddenly had a very painful, flattened tail. In the following days, that section of tail rotted and fell off. Mr. Miller not only had a shortened tail, he also had a shortened temperament. He became an angry, fighting, wild cat. He clawed and bit the dog. He pursued the other farm cats with ferocity. Soon every moving creature his size became his enemy. Even the children stayed away from him.

Whenever the family found a dead chicken or frog on the farm, they knew the critter had become a victim of Mr. Miller's wrath. Finally the family had had enough of his atrocities and got rid of him.

When I heard the story of how pain and hurt had so drastically changed the personality of this cat, I thought of similar human examples. When people lose a loved one to death or rebellion, or lose their health or wealth, or become disabled in any way, they can become permanently scarred emotionally. Some become bitter and angry toward God, toward anyone who enjoys life, or who seems more fortunate than they. Some use ugly words to claw, scratch, and bite whomever they meet. However, some become more gracious, more loving, and more caring.

I can allow adversity to use me or I can use adversity. I can permit adversity to reduce me to bitterness and unbelief, or I can turn my affliction into an exercise of faith and a means of blessing. Will my suffering humble me or harden me? Grow me or shrink me? Make me or break me? I must never allow anger, fear, bitterness, hopelessness, or depression to take up permanent residence in my heart.

O Lord, keep me from becoming like Mr. Miller, the injured cat. When the cutting winds of adversity buffet me, keep me sweet and loving and ever trusting in you. When my dreams are dashed, help me to not despair; help me to seek for grace, to find hope again. When my heart is broken, help me to give it back to you as a love token. Help me, Lord, not to faint in the day of adversity.

May my suffering become a gift to be cherished because of the way it has enhanced my relationship with God.

QUESTIONS

1. How have I shown that my strength is small or weak during this time of trouble? In what negative ways have I responded?
2. What positive effects of adversity can I observe in my life right now?
3. In what area have I shown myself strong, by God's grace, in this trial?
4. How is God sharing with me through suffering?

Book of Remembrance

Then they that feared the LORD spake often one to another: and the LORD hearkened, and heard it, and a book of remembrance was written before him for them that feared the LORD, and that thought upon his name. And they shall be mine, saith the LORD of hosts, in that day when I make up my jewels; and I will spare them, as a man spareth his own son that serveth him. Malachi 3:16–17

Someone once said, "To be religious is our highest goal." A better goal would be to seek to attain and maintain a close relationship with Christ, making that the supreme aim of our lives. May we say with Paul, "For me to live is Christ" (Philippians 1:21).

Trials, losses, and valleys should all contribute to—not distract or subtract from—this relationship. How they affect me depends on my response and my focus when life becomes difficult. These verses from Malachi suggest a number of ways I can maintain my relationship with Christ.

- Do I want the Lord to consider me? I will consider Him.
- Do I want the Lord to think on me? I will think on Him.
- Do I want the Lord to hear me? I will hear and fear Him.
- Do I want the Lord to speak of me and to me? I will speak of Him and to Him.
- Do I want the Lord to remember me? I will remember Him.
- Do I want to belong to the Lord? I will give myself to Him.

Every situation that God allows in my life is for my good. Through every circumstance, God is bringing me into a better, stronger, and more loving relationship with Him for His glory.

When I have a vital connection with Him:

- He attends to all my needs.
- He claims me for His very own.
- He knows me and loves me.
- He appreciates me. I am precious to Him—a jewel.
- He sets me apart from all others.
- He writes about me in His book of remembrance.

"The LORD is good, a strong hold in the day of trouble; and he knoweth them that trust in him" (Nahum 1:7).

God knows His own. Intimately and lovingly, personally and individually, He cares for those who commit themselves to Him. Yet I wonder, *Why must I pass through flood after flood, fire after fire, if you love me so much?*

God replies, ***My love does not remove your trial, but it assures you that I am in command of what touches you. My love does not lift you from the floodwaters, but it promises you that I am walking beside you. My love does not stop the fire, but it carries you through it.***

I created you in my image; you are mine. I understand you and remember that you are frail dust. I redeemed you with my lifeblood because I love you. I call you by name because you are precious and honorable to me. You are a special person—a peculiar treasure to me. I claim you as my child. I am your Father. Because of our relationship, I will always care for you in love. Do not be anxious or fearful. Trials are a proof of my love and a verification of your character.

Tell me, why did you become anxious? Why did you become fearful? Why can't you lean, trust, and wait on me? Why do you doubt my care? Why do you question my ways? Why do you resist my plan? Rest in my care. Trust in my ways. Yield to my plan. Submit to my heart.

His way is perfect. That should take the question out of my pain, though it does not take the pain out of my heart.

QUESTIONS

1. What is my foremost goal in life?
2. In what ways am I considering God?
3. How is God showing me that He cares for and knows me?
4. What do I think God might have written in His book of remembrance about me?

The Power of My Belief System

And Jacob their father said unto them, Me have ye bereaved of my children: Joseph is not, and Simeon is not, and ye will take Benjamin away: all these things are against me. Genesis 42:36

And God Almighty give you mercy before the man, that he may send away your other brother, and Benjamin. If I be bereaved of my children, I am bereaved. Genesis 43:14

Jacob was feeling overwhelmed with life's complexities. The family was dealing with difficulties brought about by the famine in the land. Furthermore, Jacob was still mourning the loss of his son Joseph. The reality of that grief resurfaced when Simeon was detained as a prisoner in Egypt. Now his sons were saying Benjamin must go along to Egypt the next time they went for food.

This was too much for Jacob! "All these things are against me!" he exclaimed (Genesis 42:36). Trials had torn Jacob's belief system away from its moorings. He focused on his losses and not on the power of God. His grief held him hostage and crippled his ability to move forward.

Before Jacob could take a step forward, he had to refocus on his God. "God Almighty give you mercy before the man" (Genesis 43:14). Jacob chose to change his attitude from, "All things are against me!" to confidence in the mercy of God Almighty. Jacob was still in doubt as to what would happen to his sons, but he took that step of faith, and God blessed him beyond his imagination. Joseph and Jacob were reunited!

What might have happened if Jacob had stayed in the "All things are against me" mode? What if he had refused to move ahead in faith?

Lord, I need to deal with my belief system. My mental log of losses must fade and be replaced with a mental log of your goodness and faithfulness. Life's experiences cannot be the foundation for my belief system! Your divine attributes must be the basis of my belief system if I would survive and grow through painful episodes. Help me to trace the fingerprints of your love, mercy, and grace in the agonizing experiences of life.

QUESTIONS

1. Is my belief system stable or not? What has made it unstable or what has kept it stable?

2. Do I have a mental log of losses, and do I feel that all things are against me?
3. What do I need to do to change my pattern of thinking?
4. Is God asking something of me that I do not want to do?
5. When it seems like everything is against me, it is very easy to slip off to a pity party. Have I attended my own pity party? How can I get up and leave it?

Blessings—More and More

He hath remembered his mercy and his truth toward the house of Israel: all the ends of the earth have seen the salvation of our God. Psalm 98:3

What do I remember about the Lord? What would I like Him to remember about me? How is what God remembers different from what I remember?

As humans, we remember some of the good deeds we have done for our friends. Thinking of how I helped him or her gives me a natural reason to expect help from that friend. God remembers me not only because of what He has already done for me, but because of keeping His honor and His promises.

I would become annoyed at the beggar who comes repeatedly with presumptuous confidence because he has been so often successful in getting something from me.

God, however, responds to the beggar exactly the opposite as I would. In fact, He never treats me as a beggar, but calls me a daughter. God loves to bless those who look to Him in expectation. He remembers His mercy and truth, His loving-kindness and faithfulness. He reaches out and touches my life, meeting my needs again and again with His mercy and truth.

No matter how often I come to beg, He has more mercy and truth to share with me. He promises to care for me with tender faithfulness:

"But now thus saith the LORD that created thee, O Jacob, and he that formed thee, O Israel, Fear not: for I have redeemed thee, I have called thee by thy name; thou art mine. When thou passest through the waters, I will be with thee; and through the rivers, they shall not overflow thee: when thou walkest through the fire, thou shalt not be burned; neither shall the flame kindle upon thee" (Isaiah 43:1–2).

What love!
What sacrifice!
What relationship!
What promise!

The God of love
created me in love,
redeemed me in love,
calls me by name in love,
claims me in love,
and cares for me in love.

When God hears my memories of His loving-kindness toward me, He can only pour out more. Not only my family, but also an ever-widening circle of acquaintances will recognize God's mercy and grace in my life. That is the blessing of remembering. Remembering bolsters my trust in God when more times of pain and trials come. I may need to dig a little deeper to find God's blessings of mercy and truth, but I know they are there because I have experienced them before, and I know God is faithful.

Help me, Lord, to praise you more and more. Even in the darkest night, your mercy and truth are my light.

Faith is strengthened not by striving for more faith,
but by rest in the faithfulness of God.

QUESTIONS

1. How would I feel about a beggar coming to me repeatedly because he has been successful in getting what he wanted?
2. How does God respond to me when I come to Him repeatedly?
3. What are some mercies of God that I remember and appreciate?
4. Do all my memories or facts of God's truth about myself make me happy and comfortable?

God Is Able

Wherefore, when I came, was there no man? when I called, was there none to answer? Is my hand shortened at all, that it cannot redeem? or have I no power to deliver? behold, at my rebuke I dry up the sea, I make the rivers a wilderness. Isaiah 50:2

"Surely what I have done once, I can do again!" we imagine God exclaiming incredulously. He has absolute control over all of nature. The universe submits, bends, and moves at His command. We humans too often resist and rebel against His command.

How do we account for our alienation from God in the dark times of our lives? He is not unable or unwilling! He is not powerless! He is not uncaring! If we are separated from God, the problem is ours, not God's. God has not moved away from us. God understands our feelings and carries our pain in His heart.

Let's listen to His tender questions, heeding with our hearts His gentle inquiries:

Is my hand shortened . . .

- ***That I cannot touch your broken heart with healing?***
- ***That I cannot enfold you in my arms of love?***
- ***That I cannot be a Friend in your loneliness?***
- ***That I cannot hold your hand and walk with you in the dark?***
- ***That I cannot carry your burdens?***
- ***That I cannot assuage your fears?***
- ***That I cannot offer you the flower of peace?***
- ***That I cannot carry you when you are weak?***
- ***That I cannot embrace you when you need comfort?***
- ***That I cannot wipe the worries from your forehead?***
- ***That I cannot wash the tears from your eyes?***

The heart of rest
When all without tumultuous seems—
That trusts a higher will, and deems
That higher will, not mine, the best.

O blessed life—heart, mind, and soul,
From self-born aims and wishes free,
In all at one with Deity,
And loyal to the Lord's control.

—Matson

QUESTIONS

1. If I feel alienated from God, what is the problem?
2. How do I respond to God when life goes smoothly? When things get rough?
3. Do I ever respond to God like He's disabled?
4. Often when God feels far away, people do also. Am I having other relationship problems?

God's Mercy and Truth

For the LORD is good; his mercy is everlasting; and his truth endureth to all generations. Psalm 100:5

God's goodness comes from two of His qualities: His mercy and His truth. Goodness is love, kindness, benevolence, thoughtfulness, mercy, and faithfulness. Goodness is dealing graciously with the weak, with the hurting, with those in sin, in pain, or in grief.

Well, this is not the way God is dealing with me, may be my first thought when I think about God's goodness. Where is His goodness when He devastates life with a fire, wind, or flood? Where is His kindness when He sends debilitating pain? Where is His love when He takes away a loved one in the prime of life?

God might ask, ***Who are you to pronounce me different than my eternal Word says? Who are you to decide on the length of a lifetime or the purpose of the storm or pain?***

O Lord, give me a humble, submissive heart! Keep me out of Satan's trap of self-pity and humanistic thinking. Forgive me when I forget your goodness.

The earth is full of the goodness of the Lord. I only need to open my eyes, my heart, and my mind to see and experience a full panorama of the beauty of God's goodness.

Satan delights in getting me to grieve as those who have no hope, as those who harden their hearts to God's mercy and truth. They are estranged from God's goodness, His loving-kindness and faithfulness—that is the miserable way of people without God.

The goodness of God is mercy. The goodness of God is truth. It is the strongest wall I can raise against sin. The goodness of God should lead me to repentance, and cause me to do good to others. It should inspire me to trust Him completely. The goodness of God should carry me through my grieving process and fill me with wonder at His loving-kindness and faithfulness.

When I feel out of touch with God's goodness, I imagine a week without light, sunshine, or rain; without sunrise or sunset, moon or stars; without prayer or reading God's Word; without a touch from any caring human, the beauty of nature, or a breath of fresh air; without hope of eternal life. I could not survive without even these small pieces of God's goodness.

"O give thanks unto the LORD; for he is good" (Psalm 118:1).

When we in darkness walk,
Nor feel the heavenly flame,
Then is the time to trust our God,
And rest upon His name.
—Augustus M. Toplady

QUESTIONS

1. What things in nature show me God's goodness?
2. In what ways do I doubt God's goodness?
3. In what ways do I experience God's goodness?
4. Because God is truth, I can trust Him to be good. Because He is truth, I can trust him to be merciful, forgiving, loving, kind, compassionate, and all the other things His Word says He is. What does this mean to me in my everyday life?

Who Is God?

And the LORD passed by before him, and proclaimed, The LORD, The LORD God, merciful and gracious, longsuffering, and abundant in goodness and truth, keeping mercy for thousands, forgiving iniquity and transgression and sin, and that will by no means clear the guilty; visiting the iniquity of the fathers upon the children, and upon the children's children, unto the third and to the fourth generation. Exodus 34:6–7

These verses are God's revelation of Himself. God not only revealed to Moses His name, but also His character. Jehovah is the Self-Existent God, the Eternal One, the uncreated but the Creator of all things—including my existence—on whom I am absolutely dependent.

This God is the Tender One, full of kindness and compassion. He is the Gracious One, who bestows His benefits and blessings because of His good favor, without obligation. He is the Longsuffering One, not easily provoked, but infinitely patient. He is great in mercy, and His loving-kindness is everlasting. He is the keeper of mercy. He never deserts those He loves, but is merciful to them and their children from generation to generation. He is merciful even in reminding them of their sins. He forgives iniquities, transgressions, and sins. Only He can take away our guilt by the blood of His Son. God is always just. He is all goodness. He is all truth. "Thy truth reacheth unto the clouds" (Psalm 108:4).

God Himself, the Truth, is the foundation of our trust. Without truth, God's revelation of His name and character would have no power or value.

Repeatedly the Lord reminds us of His name, His character, and His trustworthiness. Why? Sometimes all we can see is darkness and disappointment. A German artist created a painting called *Cloudland*. When the picture is viewed from a distance, it appears a mass of darkness, gloom, and clouds. However, a closer view shows that every cloud is an angel or an angel's wing. In Habakkuk 3:17–18, Habakkuk describes the barrenness he sees. "Although the fig tree shall not blossom, neither shall fruit be in the vines; the labour of the olive shall fail, and the fields shall yield no meat; the flock shall be cut off from the fold, and there shall be no herd in the stalls: yet I will rejoice in the LORD, I will joy in the God of my salvation." Everything from field to flock had failed. Yet when he adds the light of thanksgiving to the picture, the scene changes—angels' wings appear, as it were.

Doesn't this depict our sorrows and valleys? All appears as gloom and doom until we recognize the light of God's presence in the picture, and add thanksgiving to the scene. We do not understand His plan, but when we choose to accept what comes from His hand, we can trust His wisdom.

We need reminders while experiencing pain. God knows how to move us toward Him.

When I learn to rest in God and try to comprehend His loving work in my life, He proves Himself my Strength, my Song, and my Salvation. When I have faith in His faithfulness, the dark clouds become angels—angels guarding, guiding, and giving me strength in the dark moments.

It is one thing to know about God and another thing to know God.

QUESTIONS

1. What is causing the darkness and gloom that I feel today?
2. What are some thoughts or who are some people who give me courage?
3. How would I describe my battle with how I think life ought to be and how it really is?
4. How has God proven Himself trustworthy to me?
5. According to Psalm 115:11 and 13, what will God do for me when I trust and fear Him?

Search My Heart

I the LORD search the heart, I try the reins, even to give every man according to his ways, and according to the fruit of his doings. Jeremiah 17:10

Does asking to be searched make you feel uneasy? In Psalm 139:23–24, David opened his heart to be searched by God: "Search me, O God, and know my heart: try me, and know my thoughts: and see if there be any wicked way in me, and lead me in the way everlasting."

In the above verse from Jeremiah, God tells us He searches the heart—whether we invite His examination or not.

Being willing to be searched and tried by God is the path to growth and maturity. It has been said, "Growth always requires discomfort." The valley of grief or distress is certainly not a comfortable place to travel, but it is a fertile place to grow—either closer to God or further away from Him. The direction of my growth depends on whether or not my will is surrendered to God. Is my heart flexible to His will or am I easily bent out of shape? As Michael McGriffy quipped, "Blessed are the flexible, for they shall not be bent out of shape."

It is human nature to desire comfort, but when comfort becomes my highest priority, I am shamefully selfish. Did Jesus ever seek comfort while living on this earth? Truly, He had much less comfort than any of us have. He had no place to lay His head. He was constantly hounded and ridiculed by the religious leaders of His day. Jesus found comfort in healing and helping the hurting people around Him.

When we experience loss, it is natural and necessary to seek for relief from our pain. At the same time, it is appropriate to pray, *Search me, O God. Show me my selfishness in my grief. Take away my demanding spirit. Open my eyes to your plan for my life. Help me to accept this trial in a God-glorifying way. Renew and clarify my goal in life.*

Trials are also a time for me to examine my own heart before God. Am I seeking only to be comforted or am I learning to be a comforter? Am I looking for pity, or am I finding peace in God's plan? Am I rushing through the valley and ignoring His lessons? Am I walking in His light and learning what He is trying to teach me? I am, without doubt, out of my comfort zone! Is my discomfort helping me to grow?

Growth means there are some lacks in my life, some blind spots, some rough edges, and some shortcomings. Growth means I need help, and I am willing to admit it. Growth always requires discomfort.

> Even with the shadow of the cross before Him, Christ managed to look beyond the darkness of Calvary to the sun of eternity.
>
> —author unknown

QUESTIONS

1. Do I desire God to search my heart? Why? Why not?
2. What will keep me from getting bent out of shape when God brings difficulties into my life?
3. What changes am I going through that make me unhappy and uncomfortable?
4. What do I do to relieve my pain and discomfort?
5. Is my goal to be happy and comfortable, or do I have another goal? What is it?

Who Can Turn Him?

But he is in one mind, and who can turn him? and what his soul desireth, even that he doeth. For he performeth the thing that is appointed for me: and many such things are with him. Therefore am I troubled at his presence: when I consider, I am afraid of him. Job 23:13–15

"The person who concedes that God may not do for him what he desires"—fix his pain, relieve his loneliness, make his loved one well—"is farther along in his understanding of God than the one who cheerfully expects God to make everything better."[21]

A presumptuous expectation of what God will do is not faith. Moreover, faith does not insist that God perform the way I think He should.

Loretta became disillusioned with religion and distrusting of God when He failed to answer her prayers and bring back her estranged husband. What had brought her to her knees in prayer also ended up driving her away from God. She could not accept that God's working might be different from her thinking or that her husband's will might be different from her will. I am sure God desired for her husband to come back, but her husband was making his own choices. She had been so certain that if she prayed enough, surrendered to the Lord enough, and changed her life enough, the God of love would surely send her husband back home to her. But he did not come back.

O Lord, help me to remember—serving you is not about getting my way, relieving my pain, or avoiding difficult trials. Keep my faith humble enough to acknowledge your right to accomplish your purpose in the way you choose. May my faith rest in the knowledge that all blessings and all pains have passed through your perfect will before reaching me.

Job recognized God as having one mind, inflexible and changeless. He does what He will. Are these comfortable thoughts? No, not for Job in his position of immeasurable losses and not for me in my position of grief. It is normal to worry about what God will do next.

Lord, help me to understand that you are not picking on me. Like Job, I am not alone in my suffering. Hundreds of thousands of other hurting, broken hearts are suffering from all kinds of painful situations.

The world is full of misery. However, the world is also full of the beauties of

God and His loving mercy. Oh, for a heart that trustingly waits on God and does not push my will ahead of His!

> Grief drives men into habits of serious reflections,
> sharpens the understanding, and softens the heart.
> —John Adams

QUESTIONS

1. How have I tried to "turn" the mind of God?
2. When I am upset or baffled by the way God did not answer my prayer, what is my problem?
3. What might cause me to become disillusioned with religion and distrusting of God?

Rest

Let us therefore fear, lest, a promise being left us of entering into his rest, any of you should seem to come short of it. Let us labour therefore to enter into that rest, lest any man fall after the same example of unbelief. Hebrews 4:1, 11

Our wills are ours to bless or pain;
They know not rest 'till Christ doth reign.
—author unknown

"In creation, the rest of God is exhibited as a sense of power which nothing wearies."[22] God completed His glorious works in six days and saw that everything was good, and then He rested from His works and commanded man to rest. When the work is good and complete, what more is there to do but rest?

O Lord, bring my mind, body, and spirit into that rest of your power, the rest in which nothing can cause worry or make weary. That is the kind of rest that only comes through my connection with you.

My circumstances are unstable, unreliable, and painfully wearisome.

- *No rest is found in circumstances.*
- *No rest is found in things.*
- *No rest is found in people.*
- *No rest is found in finances or health.*
- *No rest is found in human thoughts and methods.*

Rest is found in you, the Creator and Giver of rest. It is indeed labor to enter into your rest, but it is worth the effort. When I come to you with my will committed totally to yours, I find rest. When I acknowledge your higher knowledge and wisdom, even in the painful experiences of life, I find rest. When I cry to you in humility and absolute dependence, I find rest.

To rest in God is to yield oneself up to the highest activity.[23]
—Andrew Murray

To will what God doth will, that is the only discipline that gives us rest.
—Francois de Malherbe

Our souls need to rest in God before our works can glorify Him.

QUESTIONS

1. What are some things that I feel at rest about?
2. What are some things that I am not at rest about?
3. What helps me to feel restful, without worry, and not weary?
4. How does my attitude affect others? Do I make others feel apprehensive or restful, sad or blessed?

God's Throne

Let us therefore come boldly unto the throne of grace, that we may obtain mercy, and find grace to help in time of need. Hebrews 4:16

What is God's throne?

To the universe, God's throne is a throne of majesty.

To the sinner, God's throne is a throne of judgment.

To the saint, God's throne is a throne of grace.

From that throne of grace flow divine mercy and sympathy.

"For we have not an high priest which cannot be touched with the feeling of our infirmities; but was in all points tempted like as we are, yet without sin" (Hebrews 4:15). Christ could be called "The Great Physician of the Nervous System."

He is touched with the feeling of the infirmities . . .

of my health,

of my temper,

of my mental capacity,

of my devotion,

of my judgment,

of my temptation,

and of my grief.

He knows, feels, and understands everything that touches me. It takes my human mind a few minutes to process that thought, and when I think I am finished, there is much more to process. In fact, I can never comprehend the depth of His feelings for me, but realizing and meditating on them greatly encourages me.

When I think of His immeasurable mercy and feeling for my infirmities, I am encouraged to come to His throne in bold confidence. Even though I do not merit God's favor and blessing, He always offers me help in time of need. Life presents many, many times of need. Grief is certainly one of those times when I must come to His throne of grace repeatedly.

How often do I feel my need not supplied because I do not come and do not ask? How often were my needs met when I came and asked?

God's capacity to feel is incalculable. He is ready to supply grace. God's storehouse of blessings is full; He loves to give.

He knows, He feels, He hears my prayer;
He holds, He lifts me from despair.
O gentle Healer, touch my heart;
Make broken pieces your work of art.

> No cloud can overshadow a true child of God
> But his faith will discern a rainbow upon it.
> —Bishop Horne

QUESTIONS

1. What are my infirmities? How am I dealing with them?
2. What does God's throne mean to me?
3. In what ways is God making broken pieces a work of art in my life?

"I AM THAT I AM"

And Moses said unto God, Who am I, that I should go unto Pharaoh, and that I should bring forth the children of Israel out of Egypt? And he said, Certainly I will be with thee; and this shall be a token unto thee, that I have sent thee: When thou hast brought forth the people out of Egypt, ye shall serve God upon this mountain. And Moses said unto God, Behold, when I come unto the children of Israel, and shall say unto them, The God of your fathers hath sent me unto you; and they shall say to me, What is his name? what shall I say unto them? And God said unto Moses, I AM THAT I AM: and he said, Thus shalt thou say unto the children of Israel, I AM hath sent me unto you. Exodus 3:11–14

The truest reality does not lie in who I am, but who God is. God declares, "I am that I am; I will be that I will be; I am because I am He that is, and was, and is to come" (see also Revelation 1:8). God, the I AM, is the Self-Existent One who never changes. Lord, help me to see and experience who you are through my valley.

When God asked Moses to lead the Israelites, Moses lost sight of the big picture, focusing on himself and his inabilities. He said:

- "Who am I that I should go?"
- "What shall I say?"
- "But they will not believe me."
- "They will not harken to my voice."
- "I am not eloquent."
- "I am slow of speech."

How did God answer Moses?

- "I send thee to Pharaoh."
- "Certainly I will be with thee."
- "Say, 'I AM hath sent me.' "
- "I am the God of your fathers."
- "This is my name forever."
- "Who made man's mouth? Have not I the Lord made it?"

In the consciousness of my smallness and inabilities, I must focus on God's greatness, power, and ability to make His strength evident through my weakness. When He assigns me a difficult path, I must lean on Him and follow in His way.

Lacerations of the heart are more painful and harder to heal than any bodily wound. Many millions before me have experienced these lacerations and have found them as overwhelming as Moses' assignment. I must focus on the Designer and Assigner, the Good Shepherd, not on the valley, the darkness, or the pain. To the great I AM I surrender my sorrow and pain, looking to Him for healing.

QUESTIONS

1. What is God asking me to do that I feel incapable of doing?
2. What is He asking me to accept that I feel unwilling to accept?
3. Who is God? Is He the great I AM in my life?
4. When I feel small, He becomes big and strong. How does that concept work out in real life?

Can I Trust the **Arm of God?**

God's arm delivered Israel out of Egypt. "The great temptations which thine eyes saw, and the signs, and the wonders, and the mighty hand, and the stretched out arm, whereby the LORD thy God brought thee out: so shall the LORD thy God do unto all the people of whom thou art afraid" (Deuteronomy 7:19).

"Thou hast scattered thine enemies with thy strong arm" (Psalm 89:10). "For he hath done marvellous things: his right hand, and his holy arm, hath gotten him the victory" (Psalm 98:1).

His arm and hand are strong. "Thou hast a mighty arm: strong is thy hand, and high is thy right hand" (Psalm 89:13).

His arm will be my strength. "With whom my hand shall be established: mine arm also shall strengthen him" (Psalm 89:21).

His arm makes Him Ruler and Shepherd. "Behold, the Lord GOD will come with strong hand, and his arm shall rule for him: behold, his reward is with him, and his work before him. He shall feed his flock like a shepherd: he shall gather the lambs with his arm, and carry them in his bosom, and shall gently lead those that are with young" (Isaiah 40:10–11).

His arm is worthy of my trust. "My righteousness is near; my salvation is gone forth, and mine arms shall judge the people; the isles shall wait upon me, and on mine arm shall they trust" (Isaiah 51:5).

His arm created all things. "I have made the earth, the man and the beast that are upon the ground, by my great power and by my outstretched arm, and have given it unto whom it seemed meet unto me" (Jeremiah 27:5).

Nothing is too hard for His arm. "Ah Lord GOD! behold, thou hast made the heaven and the earth by thy great power and stretched out arm, and there is nothing too hard for thee" (Jeremiah 32:17).

Yes, I can trust His arm. Indeed, I *must* trust His arm if my life is to be pleasing to my Creator. His is a strong, mighty, faithful, holy, gentle, loving, all-powerful arm.

> I borrowed God's hand in my sorrow
> And held it till tears went away.
> I said, "I'll return it tomorrow;
> Just let me hold on for today."

Somehow, time slipped through my fingers.
I feel that's the way that He planned.
The feel of His presence still lingers,
I can't let go of God's hand.

—author unknown

QUESTIONS

1. What has the arm of God been for me during my trials?
2. When the arm of the Lord seems short or absent, what is the problem?
3. Have I learned that I can trust God's arm?

Consider Him

For consider him that endured such contradiction of sinners against himself, lest ye be wearied and faint in your minds. Hebrews 12:3

How much have I considered Jesus during my time of trial? When life flows smoothly, I often fail to consider what Christ endured for me. When life gets rough, I sometimes wonder why He doesn't do more to help me.

Spending time considering the character of God has been very helpful on my dark days. But why have I shied away from considering Christ's death? Does it stir up too much pain? Yet all the deaths that have touched my life were very different from His death.

Jesus lived a perfect, loving life of service. Still, "the contradiction of sinners" was always before Him (see Hebrews 12:3). The scribes and Pharisees hounded His every step, every word, and every deed. He possessed no fault, but they found fault with everything about Him. He was blasphemed, falsely accused, mocked, treated shamefully, and then crucified between two criminals. His twelve followers forsook him; one denied him, and another betrayed him.

He descended from the throne of God to the grave of man.

He descended from the glories of heaven to the trials of earth.

He descended from His position of honor as the son of God to become the servant of mankind.

I have never been brought to such humility. My trials have never reached the point where I was totally forsaken by friends or dying for my faith. *O Lord, help me to keep your suffering in view. May the memory of what you endured always prod me onward lest I be weary and faint in my soul. Help me to remember "yet a little while," and the race will be over and the victory won* (Hebrews 10:37). *Help me to "lay aside every weight" and "run with patience the race that is set before [me]"* (Hebrews 12:1).

Lord, protect me under the weight of prosperity, adversity, care, sorrow, or happiness. Support me under the weight of popularity or loneliness, of busyness or the expectations of friends. Keep me from succumbing to whatever weight Satan may try to use to hamper my progress.

None of the weights put on the Savior by the human race ever hampered Him from doing His Father's will. Even the weight of the sins of the world did not kill Him; He gave His life in love on Calvary.

> Lord, should my path through suffering lie,
> Forbid it I should e'er repine;
> Still let me turn to Calvary,
> Nor heed my grief, remembering thine.[24]
>
> —Josiah Conder

QUESTIONS

1. Have I considered Christ in the light of my tribulation? How have I considered Him?
2. What weights was I dealing with before the present tribulation?
3. What weights am I dealing with presently?
4. What emotions am I dealing with? Do I feel the weight of guilt or the weight of being unforgiven?

Father of Lights

Every good gift and every perfect gift is from above, and cometh down from the Father of lights, with whom is no variableness, neither shadow of turning. James 1:17

God is the Father of lights. What a comfort for those of us who are traveling through a dark valley! God is light and the Creator of light. He spoke the stars, moon, and sun into existence. Before their creation, His very presence was the light.

The valley seems rather dark at times, but what would it be like without His presence? God is the Father of:

- Sunlight, starlight, planet light, and moonlight. Without these lights, earth would be a big, dark mass.
- Life-light. Light gives life to plants, animals, and mankind. God's love became our eternal life-light when He sent His Son to die for us. God is the life-light of the angels, for every angel is a flame of fire (Hebrews 1:7).
- Truth-light. The Word of God gives us truth-light through knowledge and wisdom. God Himself is Truth and His Word is the light-line to eternal life.
- Grace-light. Truth-light shines from the outside in while grace-light shines from the inside out. Only those who walk in God's will and live by His Holy Spirit's direction have the light of God's grace shining from their souls.
- Heaven-light. Heaven, the home of God, is full of the light of God and the Lamb. "And the city had no need of the sun, neither of the moon, to shine in it: for the glory of God did lighten it, and the Lamb is the light thereof" (Revelation 21:23). God's holiness and purity are the lights of heaven.
- Unvarying light. God's light is changeless, predictable, consistent, never wavering, sure, steady, stable, and continuous!

Lord, thank you for being the Father of lights. Help me to live, talk, and walk as a child of the Light.

QUESTIONS

1. When I contrast a dark, gloomy day with a day filled with sunshine, what does it tell me about what light does for me?
2. What are some ways I can share sunshine with others?
3. What are some ways others have shared sunshine with me?
4. How has God been my light during troubled times?
5. Does the amount of light I experience depend on my attitude? How?

God's Gifts

He that spared not his own Son, but delivered him up for us all, how shall he not with him also freely give us all things? Romans 8:32

When we were enemies to God, He spared not—did not withhold—His Son. He sent Jesus from heaven's glories to earth's dark unbelief, ridicule, slander, and death for me, the sinner. Will He not do much more for us now that we are His friends?

Jesus is the sum of all good gifts, inestimable and unspeakable. He is the greatest gift ever given. If God spared not His own Son, is there any gift He will spare for His child?

God bestows . . .

generously as a King,
tenderly as a Father,
mercifully as a Savior,
and wisely as a Good Shepherd.

God's gifts are bountifully bestowed. Every possession, every privilege, and every ability is a gift from God. On dreary mornings, let's count our gifts from God. As we do so, the Son will shine in our hearts.

In this passage, notice the words *with him*. With Christ come all other gifts. He and His gifts cannot be separated.

My position in Christ is a gift. I am a widow who is bereft of two daughters. I am learning to be thankful for these painful gifts—not thankful that I lost loved ones, but thankful for what God is teaching me through these experiences. I am also thankful that they are with Him in glory.

So what shall I do with my gifts? Shall I hide them in a dark closet? Place them on a high shelf for display? Trash them or give them away? Keep them handy and use them for the benefit of others?

When God gives us gifts He expects some return. What will I return to Him? He gives me compassion that I might be compassionate. He gives me comfort that I might comfort. He gives me help that I might help. He gives me light that I might share His light in this dark world. He meets my needs that I might commit my desires to Him.

He who his Son, most dear and beloved,
Gave up for us to die,
Shall he not all things freely give
That goodness can supply?

—author unknown

QUESTIONS

1. What are some of the gifts God has given me?
2. What am I doing with God's gifts?
3. Why does God usually satisfy needs and not fulfill wants?
4. Based on Job 23:10, what was one of Job's conclusions about the suffering he endured?

The Secret of the Lord

What man is he that feareth the LORD? The secret of the LORD is with them that fear him. Psalm 25:12, 14

"Find me such a man [who fears God], and I will tell you how it will fare with him. God will reveal Himself to him otherwise than He does to the world. Between them, there is sympathy and sweet accord. God opens His mind to those who love Him. He lets them into His secrets."[25]

God favors the person who fears Him because that person lives to bring glory to His name. The Father and the Son "will come unto him, and make [their] abode with him" (John 14:23). God teaches him and enlightens him, leading him in paths of righteousness.

God reveals Himself to His faithful saints. He shows His love and care for them in many ways.

God gave Joseph courage and determination when he faced the temptation of Potiphar's wife (Genesis 39:7–12). Later, Joseph displayed patience and wisdom as he suffered in jail, imprisoned for crimes he did not commit (39:21–23). God gave him grace to forgive his heartless brothers.

God revealed His strength, power, and courage to David when he went out to meet Goliath (1 Samuel 17:20–51).

God gave Elijah boldness to challenge the worshipers of Baal on Mount Carmel (1 Kings 18:17–39).

God gave the three Hebrew boys fearless courage in the face of fire (Daniel 3:1–30).

God gave Daniel a faithful, trusting heart when he was thrown into the lions' den (Daniel 6:3–23).

These men all knew the secret of the Lord because they had a reverent fear of the Lord. They knew His strength, power, faithfulness, and wisdom in everyday life. When life threw them a curve, they were ready to meet the challenge! Their faith and trust was anchored in a never changing God. Dozens of other Bible characters knew the secret of the Lord. May they challenge us daily to remain in the favor of God by fearing Him.

Help me, Lord, to be aware of the secrets you are revealing to me, not to inflate my pride, but to increase my humility, meekness, and usefulness.

Courage, brother, do not stumble;
Though thy path be dark as night
There's a star to guide the humble;
Trust in God, and do the right.

Some will hate thee, some will love thee,
Some will flatter, some will slight;
Cease from man, and look above thee;
Trust in God, and do the right.

—Norman McLeod

The size of the storm you can survive is determined
by how well you are anchored.

—author unknown

QUESTIONS

1. In what ways does my life show that I fear the Lord?
2. In what ways does my life reveal my lack of the fear of the Lord?
3. What special things has God done in the lives of people I know who fear Him?
4. What special things has God done for me? How aware am I of His work in my life?

Our Father

Like as a father pitieth his children, so the LORD pitieth them that fear him. For he knoweth our frame; he remembereth that we are dust. Psalm 103:13–14

God is indeed a heavenly Father who loves His frail children—the ones who fear Him—and attends tenderly to their needs. Do I have the wisdom to fear the Lord?

The beginning of wisdom is not found in keen insight, in extensive experience, or in prominent schools, but in the temperament of reverence and awe toward God.

The fear of God includes "belief in God, knowledge of God, recognition of the claims of God, awe of the power and holiness of God, and the cherished sense of the presence of God."[26]

On my own I cannot direct my life aright. I make unwise choices, say unwise things, and think unwise thoughts. As someone said, "Life is only ordered aright when God orders it." Let me never forget that fact!

My life right now, Lord, seems very out of order. My life is uncomfortable, painful, lonely, and distressing when I focus on myself. When I focus on you, I find security, calmness, and hope—hope that you are ordering my life aright even when it feels like it is crumbling around me.

Because you are divine, you know how to deal with my humanity. Thank you, Lord, for being who you are. Thank you for remembering my dust-built frame which often shakes, quakes, crumbles, and stumbles during trials. In love and mercy you scoop me up and put me back together again in a form more akin to your image. How many times you will do this till I pass into glory, I do not know. I just want to thank you for continuing to work on me.

Losses, however painful, are only temporary.
Who I become during my loss is enduring.
—author unknown

QUESTIONS

1. Do my behavior and attitudes reflect the fear of God?
2. How is my life out of order and distressing right now?
3. How does God accept my humanity? When I fail, does He make excuses for my bad choices? Do I?

The Divine Touch

And the LORD said unto Satan, Hast thou considered my servant Job, that there is none like him in the earth, a perfect and an upright man, one that feareth God, and escheweth evil? Job 1:8

Have you ever stopped to thank God for:
His divine Fatherhood,
His divine patience,
His divine mercy,
His divine pity,
His divine knowledge,
His divine consideration,
His divine thoughts,
and His divine care?

Job experienced the touch of the Divine, a touch he was partly aware of but did not understand. Only when it brought great sorrow and pain did he begin to question this touch.

- Divine observation—God saw the character of Job. He was responsive to Job's devotion. He called Job by name (Job 1:8).
- Divine admiration—God respected and admired His servant's piety and worth. He called Job an upright and perfect man (1:8).
- Divine affection—God spoke of Job with love, calling him His servant (1:8).
- Divine protection—God placed a hedge of His protecting power around Job (1:10).
- Divine blessing—God had blessed Job with many material blessings. He had blessed him with a wife and children. He had blessed him with health (1:10).
- Divine permission—Job's trials came by divine permission and were controlled by divine power (1:12). God limited Satan's power.

Can I look through my trial and see the work of the divine Lord? Can I feel His divine touch above and over and through my pain?

Perhaps God sees me as a candidate to demonstrate the power of His love and grace through trial. Always God sees us as candidates for perfecting by fire through trial. Always we can decrease in our focus on self and grow in our focus on God, and trials are the fastest way to do so.

Job was not necessarily aware of God's divine observation, admiration, affection, protection, or permission, but he likely felt the divine blessing of God. He was not living in known sin, so he may have assumed he was experiencing God's divine care. Yet, there was so much he did not know or understand about God's careful attention to his life.

Help me, Lord, to rest in the fact that you are so much more involved in my life than I know. You really do love me and take care of me. You truly do have a divine plan for my pain.

> God harrows our souls, making us long for something we cannot have, in order to reveal to us what He wants us to have, which in the long run is far better.[27]
>
> —Elisabeth Elliot

QUESTIONS

1. What might God observe about me—my lacks and my needs, my strong points?
2. How has God shown His affection for me?
3. How have I been assured of God's protection?
4. What circumstances over which I have no control has God allowed into my life?

God's Correction

The LORD is merciful and gracious, slow to anger, and plenteous in mercy. He will not always chide: neither will he keep his anger for ever. Psalm 103:8–9

Chiding, but not continually chiding—"He will not always chide" (Psalm 103:9). One prophet prayed, "O Lord, correct me, but with judgment." Or as the *World English Bible* puts it, "Yahweh, correct me, but in measure"[28] (Jeremiah 10:24). A great danger for those who are in a position of authority over others is the potential for chastening excessively.

Parents, teachers, ministers, and police officers all have been known to over-punish at times. How do they determine how much punishment, how much chiding is necessary for each offense? Unrestrained feelings cause over-chiding. Physical and emotional exhaustion can cause poor judgment and anger, resulting in too much chastisement.

With God, there is no danger of over-correction or under-correction. God is never carried away by His feelings. He makes no poor judgments or inaccurate evaluations. He is the wise, powerful, and self-restrained One. God knows when to start and when to stop His chastisement, because He knows what it will take to get the end result He desires.

God has put strict limitation on His chidings, and yet He accomplishes an "exceeding and eternal weight of glory," by these "light afflictions" (2 Corinthians 4:17).

No, these afflictions do not seem light while I am in the midst of them, but I will not consider the pain I have suffered when I enter into eternal joy in God's presence. God is shaping me into His image. God's chiding is my assurance of His great love for me. He will not allow my self-willfulness to ruin me. He is the all-wise Giver—even in chiding.

We should always be mindful of this truth: "He hath not dealt with us after our sins; nor rewarded us according to our iniquities" (Psalm 103:10). If God dealt with us according to our sins, we would not be alive. This verse helps us understand God's chastisements as light afflictions. The measure of God's divine dealing with man is not the same measure as man's dealing with fellowmen.

Man deals with sins; God deals with sinners, not merely sin. A drunken man may be jailed because he ran a stoplight and hit another man. God looks at the drunk and sees his inner need and works on that.

God considers the weakness of human frailty. He remembers that we are but dust. In His wisdom and righteousness, the measure of His divine dealings is always accurate and merciful.

Mercy and justice are God's standard of measure.

Trouble never comes to a man unless she brings a nugget of gold in her hand.

—Lettie Cowman

QUESTIONS

1. Do I remember a time when I felt unjustly or overly punished by my parents or by God?
2. Have I ever unjustly or overly punished someone under my authority?
3. If I could choose whether my correction came from a human or God, which would I choose? Why?
4. How can I deal with my feeling that I have had more than my share of God's chastisements, while others seem to go untouched?

The Voice of the Lord

The voice of the LORD is upon the waters: the God of glory thundereth: the LORD is upon many waters. Psalm 29:3

Psalm 29 describes the voice of the Lord in a thunderstorm. What do I feel, see, and hear in a storm? What does it inspire in me? In this verse, I see huge, dark clouds filled with water rolling and crashing—reverberating the sound of the Lord's strength and care. C. Short said that the thunderstorm "inspires the common mind with fear. It rouses the scientific mind with inquiry. It inflames the imagination of the poetic mind. It fills the devout mind with the spirit of worship of our great Creator."[29]

"The voice of the LORD is powerful" (29:4). That voice booms forth with power and authority.

"The voice of the LORD is full of majesty" (29:4). That same voice says, "Peace, be still" (Mark 4:39).

"The voice of the LORD breaketh the cedars" (29:5). With thunder and lightning comes the wind. The wind bends, breaks, and sometimes violently rips out trees. The Lord who planted them also destroys them by His voice. That same voice said, "Let the earth bring forth grass, the herb yielding seed, and the fruit tree yielding fruit after his kind" (Genesis 1:11).

"The voice of the LORD divideth the flames of fire" (Psalm 29:7). God's voice sends out forked lightening in all directions. That voice also said, "Fear thou not; for I am with thee" (Isaiah 41:10).

"The voice of the Lord shaketh the wilderness" (Psalm 29:8). His voice causes the buildings to shake and the ground to vibrate in the blast of thunder. That same voice says, "Be still, and know that I am God" (Psalm 46:10).

The voice of the Lord is fearful—yet it gives me courage. It is powerful—and it strengthens me. It rips apart—yet it unifies and recreates. It shakes and causes to tremble—yet it comforts and calms.

The Eye of the Storm

Fear not that the whirlwind shall carry thee hence,
Nor wait for its onslaught in breathless suspense,
Nor shrink from the whips of the terrible hail,
But pass through the edge to the heart of the gale.

For there is a shelter, sun lighted and warm,
And Faith sees her God through the eye of the storm.
The passionate tempest with rush and wild roar
And threatening of evil may beat on the shore,

The waves may be mountains, the fields battle plains,
And the earth be immersed in a deluge of rains,
Yet, the soul, stayed on God, may sing bravely its psalm,
For the heart of the storm is the center of calm.

Let hope be not quenched in the blackness of night
Though the cyclone awhile may have blotted the light,
For behind the great darkness the stars ever shine,
And the light of God's heavens, His love shall make thine.

Let no gloom dim thine eyes, but uplift them on high,
To the face of thy God and the blue of His sky.
The storm is thy shelter from danger and sin,
And God Himself takes thee for safety within;

The tempest with Him passeth into deep calm,
And the roar of the winds is the sound of a psalm.
Be glad and serene when the tempest clouds form;
God smiles on His child in the eye of the storm.

—author unknown

QUESTIONS

1. What does a thunderstorm arouse in my mind—awe or fear?
2. Have I heard the voice of the Lord in the storms of life?

Christ in Me

Whereof I am made a minister, according to the dispensation of God which is given to me for you, to fulfil the word of God; even the mystery which hath been hid from ages and from generations, but now is made manifest to his saints: to whom God would make known what is the riches of the glory of this mystery among the Gentiles; which is Christ in you, the hope of glory. Colossians 1:25–27

The mystery of the riches of Christ's glory is indeed a mystery to all God's children. God has some strange ways to bring about His glory in the lives of His people. God uses some unexplainable and incomprehensible means to accomplish His purpose—Christ in you—Christ in me. Only when Christ is in us can we live in the hope of glory.

What is life without hope? Nothing! What is darkness without light? Nothing! What is death without resurrection? Nothing! What am I without Christ in me? Nothing!

When I have Christ in me, I have the hope of glory because Christ is the hope of glory. The anticipation of glory motivates me to keep climbing onward and upward.

However, what is my incentive when life becomes horrifying and dreadfully agonizing? How do I find Christ in me when it feels like He is thousands of miles across the globe? This is what I think of as the "trial of your faith"—when we face grief or some other horrific trial, we often feel like God has moved miles away. The truth of the matter is, my faith has shriveled, and I have moved away.

"That the trial of your faith, being much more precious than of gold that perisheth, though it be tried with fire, might be found unto praise and honour and glory at the appearing of Jesus Christ" (1 Peter 1:7). It is Christ's desire that in the darkest time of trial our faith would bring praise, honor, and glory to Him.

A time of trial is truly a time of examination. How can I praise the Lord even in difficulty? How can I honor His reputation and image in me? How can I, in my dark picture of loss, display the light of His glory? Is Christ truly in me, or am I suffocating in my loss? Am I finding His grace sufficient in this trial? Am I willing to surrender to His plan? Is He my personal God and not just an ancestral figure? Is He my life and not just a bandage with which I try to cover my wound?

A time of trial is a time to find out who God is to me and a time to build my faith. God is great. God is good. God is merciful. God is faithful. God is true. What I believe about God is of utmost importance.

> The light of nature, the light of science, and the light of reason,
> are but as darkness compared with the divine light
> which shines only from the words of God.[30]
>
> —John R. Lord

> Life is God's gift to us.
> What we do with it is our gift to Him.

QUESTIONS

1. What evidence do I have that Christ is in me?
2. What are my trials of faith at present?
3. Am I passing the examination of my trial? What examination questions might I be failing or needing help on?
4. What in God's creation demonstrates His glory most clearly to me?
5. How do God's dealings with me display His glory?

The Artist

Woe unto him that striveth with his Maker! Let the potsherd strive with the potsherds of the earth. Shall the clay say to him that fashioneth it, What makest thou? or thy work, He hath no hands? Isaiah 45:9

The artist never creates a masterpiece by haphazardly splashing colors across the canvas—unless he is creating modern art. Instead, the artist mixes colors, brushes, dabs, and scrapes until the picture reaches the perfection he desires.

The sculptor cannot form a beautiful, realistic statue with the rough blows of a hammer only. He will use the sculptor's chisel and carefully shape the image he carries in his mind's eye. He will chip, chop, and chisel day by day, week by week, and sometimes month by month to capture the perfection he envisions.

Lord, I am no less a work of art, being mixed, brushed, scraped, chopped, chipped, and chiseled by you. You send trials, joys, and sorrows, to flatten, smooth, and soften the rough corners of my character. It is not my business to question your work of art. It is not my business to mistrust the shaping by your hands. It is not my business to doubt the value of the chipped and chiseled edges. My concern is simply to allow you to do your work without my resistance.

Lord, prevent me from striving with my Maker. You are the Potter; I am the clay. You are the Sculptor; I am the sculpture. You are the Artist; I am the portrait. You are the Savior; I am the sinner. You are the Master; I am the servant.

The Master's Touch

In the still lute, the music lies unheard;
In the rough marble, beauty hides unseen
To make the music and the beauty, needs
The Master's touch, the Sculptor's chisel keen.

Great Master, touch us with thy skillful hand
Let not the music that is in us die!
Great Sculptor, hew and polish us; not let,
Hidden and lost, thy form within us lie.

Spare not the stroke! Do with us as thou wilt!
Let there be naught unfinished, broken, marred:
Complete thy purpose, that we may become
Thy perfect image, thou our God and Lord!

—Horatius Bonar

QUESTIONS

1. What is God using to shape me and make of me a piece of art?
2. In what ways might I be striving with my Maker?
3. What did God use to shape the Bible characters Moses, Joseph, Daniel, and David?

Guidance

Thou shalt guide me with thy counsel, and afterward receive me to glory. Whom have I in heaven but thee? and there is none upon earth that I desire beside thee. My flesh and my heart faileth: but God is the strength of my heart, and my portion for ever. Psalm 73:24-26

I need guidance because . . .

I do not know the future. God has given me foresight to see the possible outcome of many things, but human foresight is often faulty. The unexpected happens; the unplanned comes; the unwelcomed occurs; what is my next move? How do I deal with the trial that is dropped into my lap, or the unexpected blessing that is handed me?

I need a living connection with the all-knowing God. He knows the future as well as the present. He sees plainly the path ahead, and He understands the direction I should take in order to end up where He wants me. He knows the end from the beginning.

I need guidance because . . .

I sometimes judge wrongly. It matters not how correct I think my decision, or how comfortable I feel about a choice—my judgment could be very wrong. My mind is finite. My knowledge is limited.

My just and holy God knows my weaknesses and foresees the pitfalls Satan has set before me. I need His wisdom in every decision. His mind is infinite. His understanding is unlimited. He works only for the best for me.

I need guidance because . . .

I lack faith and understanding. I see my trials or blessings through human eyes. I feel my joy or pain through human emotions. I question God's righteousness and goodness through human thinking.

The thoughts of God are far above my thoughts. His unchanging faithfulness and compassionate goodness are trustworthy and always right. My eternal good is the desire of His heart.

O Lord, I need your Spirit to open my eyes, control my emotions, and direct my thoughts. I need the guidance and counsel you have promised me. Help me to follow the advice, plan, and purpose of your calling. There is no help on earth for me. You alone are my help and strength.

Strength is born in the deep silence of long-suffering hearts;
not amidst joy.[31]
—Felicia Hemans

It is not what I have, but whom.

QUESTIONS

1. In what situations do I know I need the guidance of God?
2. How is my knowledge of the future shortsighted?
3. In what ways might my judgment be wrong or lacking?
4. How is my faith and understanding lacking?
5. When I have made wrong choices, what are some of the consequences I have experienced?

No One but You

When I cry unto thee, then shall mine enemies turn back: this I know; for God is for me. Psalm 56:9

No one knows the enemies I face, the fear, desperation, guilt, hopelessness, and aloneness—but you, O Lord, know!

No one sees the flood of my tears—but you, O Lord, see!

No one hears my cries of desperation—but you, O Lord, hear!

No one feels the emptiness and agony in my heart—but you, O Lord, feel!

No one is aware of the questions, the guilt, and hopelessness of my thoughts—but you, O Lord, are aware!

No one understands the confusion of my mind—but you, O Lord, understand!

No one considers the pains pulsating through my body—but you, O Lord, consider!

No one recognizes my feelings of uselessness and lack of purpose—but you, O Lord, recognize!

No one discerns the depth of my down times—but you, O Lord, discern!

No one realizes the pain thoughtless people have inflected—but you, O Lord, realize!

No one comprehends the disruptions, changes, and abnormalities in my life—but you, O Lord, comprehend!

No one imagines the effort to put on a happy facade, the pressure to conform to people's expectations—but you, O Lord, imagine!

No one knows and forgives all my failures—but you, O Lord, know and forgive!

No one has what I need to see me through this valley experience—but you, O Lord, have everything I need and more!

QUESTIONS

1. What are my enemies, imagined or real?
2. What is my list of, "No one but God knows"?
3. I can thank God for His shielding love. Would I really want everyone to know what He knows about me?
4. In what ways has God proven Himself faithful to me during my times of trouble?

The Lord Is Good

The LORD is good, a strong hold in the day of trouble; and he knoweth them that trust in him. Nahum 1:7

O taste and see that the LORD is good: blessed is the man that trusteth in him. Psalm 34:8

The LORD is good to all: and his tender mercies are over all his works. Psalm 145:9

Am I thoroughly convinced that God is good? If I am, I will find Him my stronghold in the day of trouble. I will flee to Him when my heart is breaking. He is my strength when my spirit is overcome with sorrow. He is right when everything seems wrong. His mercy is eternal when earth life is transitory. He is accessible to all who trust in Him. He is an impregnable fortress; no enemy can prevail against Him. His hiding place is sufficient for all my needs. His objective is to take me from guilt to pardon, from sinfulness to cleansing, from anxiety to peace, from weakness to strength, from fear to trust, from unbelief to faith. He is all I need.

He knows those who trust in Him. He intimately and lovingly regards those who commit themselves to Him. He will tenderly care for personal concerns and promote His purpose in every individual who trusts Him wholeheartedly.

What an awesome, humbling thought—I am special to God! Even though there are millions of other humans whom God takes care of, He sees, hears, cares about, and supplies my needs. He knows my thoughts, and He thinks of me.

Because God is good, I can trust His plan for me to work out for good even though my circumstances seem wrong, injurious, and detrimental.

Lord, help me to trust even when it is the most difficult thing to do. Perform your good work in my heart and mind. Help me to adjust my attitudes toward my losses, my pain, my loneliness, and my grief. Cause my attitudes to be conformed to your thoughts, your plan, and your good purpose toward me. As I become more thoroughly convinced of your goodness, I will begin to see my pain as part of your plan for my good.

QUESTIONS

1. Have I ever thought, "God is too busy to care about me"?
2. How do I truly feel about God's goodness?
3. What Bible verse helps me understand that I am special to God?

Adversity

Why dost thou shew me iniquity, and cause me to behold grievance? Art thou not from everlasting, O LORD my God, mine Holy One? we shall not die. O LORD, thou hast ordained them for judgment; and, O mighty God, thou hast established them for correction. Habakkuk 1:3, 12

God is eternal; His purpose will be fulfilled.

God is holy; evil cannot be victorious.

God is righteous; His judgment is just.

God is immortal; we shall not die.

God is almighty; He has established life's adversities for our correction.

God's chastisements are not sent to sink our ship on life's sea, but to give us buoyancy and keep us afloat in the right direction.

What do adversities teach me?

- They teach me not to rely on my own thinking but to wait on the will and plan of my Creator.
- They cause me to reflect on my shortcomings and failures; they point out my strengths and weaknesses.
- They remind me of God's superior knowledge and purpose.
- They make me more receptive to the voice of God's Spirit.
- They elevate my thoughts from the temporal and material to the spiritual and eternal.
- They drive me to my knees and to God's Word for comfort and guidance, thus bringing me into closer fellowship with God.

Not all the trials of life are chastisements from God's hand. Disease, death, and most of my trials are the natural result of living in a sin-cursed world. However, my almighty God is able to use difficulties to promote spiritual growth. "My brethren, count it all joy when ye fall into divers temptations; knowing this, that the trying of your faith worketh patience" (James 1:2–3). We learn more about the ways of God through our trials than we do through the blessings.

We need these threshings of the inner spiritual man in order that the chaff may be separated from the wheat, and we become thus prepared for the heavenly garner. Let us accept all our griefs as precious tokens of the divine Father's love, and make them our convoy to bear us to Him.[32]

—S. D. Hillman

For all that in this world is great and gay,
Doth as a vapor vanish and decay.[33]

—Edmund Spenser

It does not matter what you think about how life ought to be, for you must learn to live with life how it really is.

QUESTIONS

1. What are my adversities teaching me?
2. What trial am I thanking God for and counting it all joy?
3. How can I determine if my trial is from God or caused by Satan?

The Character of God

Thy mercy, O LORD, is in the heavens; and thy faithfulness reacheth unto the clouds. Thy righteousness is like the great mountains; thy judgments are a great deep: O LORD, thou preservest man and beast. How excellent is thy lovingkindness, O God! therefore the children of men put their trust under the shadow of thy wings. Psalm 36:5-7

When I start feeling down, it is time to consider the inexhaustible fullness of the character of God. Psalm 36 contrasts the wickedness of the wicked with the goodness of God. The media, billboards, and newspapers all display the wickedness around me. Frequently I need to withdraw from the evil that surrounds me, envelop myself in God's Word, and renew my mind with the goodness of God. Psalm 36 is a good starting place!

- God's mercy—His loving-kindness—extends to the skies, mountaintops, and even the angels (Psalm 36:5).
- His faithfulness reaches to the clouds—God's dwelling place (36:5). "Hath he said, and shall he not do it? or hath he spoken, and shall he not make it good?" (Numbers 23:19).
- His judgments are a great deep—a depth of mystery, unsearchable, past finding out (Psalm 36:6).
- He preserves man and beast (36:6). Man cannot understand the providential care of God for all His creatures, but we should notice and appreciate it.
- How precious is His steadfast love! (36:7). Have I thanked Him today for His patience with me? Have I told Him I love Him?
- Because of His great goodness, we—weak, frail, and sinful humankind—find courage by placing our trust in Him, resting in the shadow of His wings (36:7).
- God is the fountain of life (36:9). He gives and takes according to His plan.
- He is light and in Him is no darkness at all (1 John 1:5). In His light, we have light and guidance (Psalm 36:9).

O my soul, rest in the character of God!

> No voice of prayer to thee can rise,
> But swift as light thy love replies;
> Not always what we ask, indeed,
> But, O most Kind! What most we need.
>
> —Harriet M. Kimball

QUESTIONS

1. What do I do when the world's sinfulness almost overwhelms me at times?
2. What are some things I can do to keep my mind pure and free from the sin all around me?
3. In what ways have I failed God during my tribulation?
4. How has God shown His goodness and power in my life?

Laid in Iron

He sent a man before them, even Joseph, who was sold for a servant: whose feet they hurt with fetters: he was laid in iron: until the time that his word came: the word of the LORD tried him. Psalm 105:17–19

Joseph's feet were hurt with fetters, and his heart was broken with betrayal. His jealous brothers sold him as a slave. The false accusations of Potiphar's lustful wife landed him in prison. The carefree butler, released from prison, forgot Joseph.

Joseph's hopes were high; he anticipated getting out of prison on the butler's good word. Perhaps he dreamed of returning home to his father. However, God had other plans.

Joseph waited and waited. Two long, disappointing years passed, but they were not wasted years. They were years of learning the discipline of faithfulness, usefulness, courage, forgiveness, contentment, and patience.

Had Joseph chosen to spend those years blaming his brothers, Potiphar's wife, and the butler, he would never have reached the palace. To move from pit to prison to palace was a painfully long process, yet it was an enlarging and strengthening experience.

During those years of waiting he was laid in chains of iron. God was working out His purpose and plan through the discipline of trial. Joseph was developing a sterling character with unshakable strength. He was being molded into a mighty deliverer. He provided salvation for his family during the years of extended famine. He was the first leader of the budding nation of Israel and did not even know it.

What had God's word been to Joseph in his teens when he had dreamed that his brothers and father would bow before him? How many years did it take until it came to pass? Did Joseph ever wish that the word of the Lord had never come to him? What amazing wonders the hand of God and the word of the Lord worked through pain in the life of Joseph!

"O my soul, quietly wait while God does His work. The sorrows, the disappointments, the shattered dreams, the darkness are all a part of His plan to impart inner strength, the courage that will keep me on the right path and bring glory to God."

QUESTIONS

1. Joseph had every reason to be disgruntled and discouraged, but he was not. Based on Joseph's story in Genesis 37, 39–40, what was his attitude? What kept him headed in the right direction?
2. What recurring phrase is found throughout the story of Joseph?
3. What difficult people or hard circumstance is God using to help me grow? Am I laid in iron?

Facts or Feelings?

Therefore I will look unto the LORD; I will wait for the God of my salvation: my God will hear me. Rejoice not against me, O mine enemy: when I fall, I shall arise; when I sit in darkness, the LORD shall be a light unto me. Micah 7:7–8

Shakespeare's character, Claudius, observed, "When sorrows come, they come not single spies, but in battalions" (*Hamlet*, 4.5.78–79). The same could be said of fear and worry. Satan is a master supplier of fears and worries, and at times, I am a master multiplier! How often do I suffer needlessly because I entertain groundless fears and worries? Life supplies sufficient "real" sorrows and fears, without my imagination adding to them. *Help me, Lord, to leave the unknown to you! Help me to look to you and wait for you as Micah described in this passage.*

"I will look unto the LORD" (Micah 7:7)—as if posted on a watchtower to look out for help. I will look with hope. **God is my refuge!**

"I will wait for the God of my salvation" (Micah 7:7)—with longing, trust, and patience. I will quietly endure with calm submission, drawing hope and strength from my relationship with God. **God is my salvation!**

"My God will hear me" (Micah 7:7)—He will answer. "He will be very gracious unto thee at the voice of thy cry; when he shall hear it, he will answer thee" (Isaiah 30:19). **God is my help!**

Satan, my enemy, seeks to devour my faith, hope, courage, strength, and dependence on God. In spite of his attacks, "When I fall, I shall arise" (Micah 7:8). When I have suffered calamity and loss, I will seek the Lord and I shall live (Amos 5:4). **God is my deliverer!**

When I sit in darkness, "the LORD shall be a light unto me" (Micah 7:8)—His unchanging love and care provide light in the darkest night. He will give me discernment to distinguish facts from fears, concern from worry. **The Lord is my light!**

Keep me, O God, from being a captive of my fears and worries.

The eagle that soars at great altitudes does not worry about how it will cross a river.

—Lettie Cowman

QUESTIONS

1. Have I ever worried about things that never happened?
2. Arthur Somers Roche said, "Worry is a thin stream of fear trickling through the mind. If encouraged, it cuts a channel into which all other thoughts are drained." What does this quote mean to me?
3. How has God been my refuge? my salvation? my help? my deliverer? my light?
4. Has there been a time when I felt God was not there for me?

Rise Up and Walk

And a certain man lame from his mother's womb was carried, whom they laid daily at the gate of the temple which is called Beautiful, to ask alms of them that entered into the temple. Then Peter said, Silver and gold have I none; but such as I have give I thee: In the name of Jesus Christ of Nazareth rise up and walk. Acts 3:2, 6

Life abounds with stark contrasts: rich/poor, filled/starving, fat/thin, sick/well, thriving/withering, alive/dead, loss/gain, ugly/beautiful. Peter and John faced some of these contrasts as they entered the temple. At the temple gate known as Beautiful, the entrance for devout people, lay a crippled, poor, perhaps dirty, beggar. What a distracting sight to behold just when they were going to worship the great God of heaven! Yet, is that not the sight God beholds when He looks down and sees us, poor dirty sinners bowing before the holy, almighty God? When we come, Jesus offers forgiveness and restoration, pardon and peace, help and hope.

Peter's testimony to the people who looked on in wonder at this restored beggar was, "The faith which is by [Jesus] hath given him this perfect soundness in the presence of you all" (Acts 3:16).

How often do I need God's restoring touch in my body, mind, and heart, and His words, "Rise up and walk"!

O Lord, grief has laid me low. Pain has crippled me! I need your touch that gives forgiveness and restoration, pardon and peace, help and hope. I desire to be made as whole as the crippled beggar who went walking, and leaping, and praising God. I want people to be amazed, to wonder at your work of great grace and mercy in my life. Surely something beautiful must come out of this terrible pain. You promised to give "beauty for ashes, the oil of joy for mourning, the garment of praise for the spirit of heaviness" (Isaiah 61:3).

A. W. Tozer said, "Wisdom, among other things, is the ability to devise perfect ends and to achieve those ends by the most perfect means."[34] Such is the wisdom of God. He sees the end from the beginning! He sees everything in focus in relation to everything else. Tozer also said, "All God's acts are done in perfect wisdom."[35] Can I trust His wisdom in the valley? Can I believe that in His wise timing, He will make me whole?

Lord, you are holy, righteous, all-knowing, and wise. When I cannot understand your plan or see where you are taking me next, you seem to say, ***Who I AM is all that needs to matter to you, for there rests your hope and your peace. I will do what I will do, and it will all come to light at last, but how I do it is my secret. Trust me, and be not afraid. In my perfect, wise timing, I will cause you to rise up and walk.***

> Let Him lead thee blindfold onwards,
> Love needs not to know
> Children who the Father leadeth
> Ask not where they go.
> Though the path be all unknown,
> Over moor and valley low.[36]
>
> —Gerhard Tersteegen

QUESTIONS

1. All losses—loss of home, health, wealth, or loved one—bring sharp contrasts, before and after contrasts. What contrasts am I dealing with?
2. In what ways am I like the beggar at the temple gate?
3. What kind of healing do I need before I can move forward?
4. Do I truly desire to go walking, and leaping, and praising God, or would I rather limp, hobble, and collect sympathy and pity?

Go Forward

And the LORD said unto Moses, Wherefore criest thou unto me? speak unto the children of Israel, that they go forward. Exodus 14:15

Before the command to move forward, there first must be a time to "fear not," a time to "stand still"—calm the inner turmoil—"and see the salvation of the Lord," and a time to "hold your peace" (Exodus 14:13–14). Then comes the command to "go forward." In the account in Exodus 14, what options did the children of Israel have? To move backward would be to fall into the hands of the Egyptians. To move forward would be to drown in the Red Sea. To remain "glued to the spot" would be to be captured and returned to Egypt. Human eyes saw no escape. However, God had a plan at the Red Sea, as He always does when we come to the end of our resources.

When God says, "Go forward," He has a plan of deliverance. What were the objectives of this Red Sea test?

- Act in obedience—the people moved forward and the sea parted and they walked on dry ground.
- Depend on God—they had no resources, no plausible plan, no options except dependence on God.
- Grow in faith—who could doubt the power of a God who piled up the water and made them a path through the sea?
- Gain a song—a great song of deliverance, commitment, and praise was sung by the delivered.

Rebellious Jonah, having first flagrantly disobeyed God's command to move forward, experienced God's deliverance out of the depths of the sea. "And said, I cried by reason of mine affliction unto the LORD, and he heard me; out of the belly of hell cried I, and thou heardest my voice. For thou hadst cast me into the deep, in the midst of the seas; and the floods compassed me about: all thy billows and thy waves passed over me. Then I said, I am cast out of thy sight; yet I will look again toward thy holy temple" (Jonah 2:2–4).

Peter was able to move forward on the sea while his eyes were on Jesus. When he looked at the storm, he began to sink. Then in great fright, he found the hand of Jesus on the wild sea. "But when he saw the wind boisterous, he was afraid; and beginning to sink, he cried, saying, Lord, save me. And immediately Jesus stretched forth his hand, and caught him, and said unto him, O thou of little faith, wherefore didst thou doubt?" (Matthew 14:30–31).

Our sea may be rough, the waves boisterous, and the wind wild. But what a lesson for us when our way is obstructed by the Red Sea of grief or any other Red Sea! We cannot move backward in grief or we will die there. We cannot jump ahead and bypass the dark valley without finding ourselves in deep trouble, again facing the darkness we tried to avoid. We cannot stand still in the valley, or Satan will overcome us. We must move forward!

God has a plan of deliverance for us. His objectives are much the same as they were for the Israelites, with some added objectives according to our individual need.

When God puts an obstacle in our way, let's seek His plan of deliverance and move forward in obedience, dependence, faith, and thanksgiving.

QUESTIONS

1. What might have been Israel's thoughts at the Red Sea? What might have been the Egyptians' thoughts at the Red Sea?
2. Jonah thought he could run away from God. What was wrong with his thoughts?
3. Peter thought he could walk on the water in his own strength, and he did for a short time. What was wrong with his thoughts?
4. What is my Red Sea right now?
5. How can I come to the point of moving forward?

Where Is My Focus?

All things are possible to him that believeth. Mark 9:23

> Got any rivers you think are uncrossable?
> Got any mountains you cannot tunnel through?
> God specializes in things thought impossible!
> He does the things others cannot do.
>
> —Oscar C. Eliason

Whether I struggle with the fear of losing a daughter to cancer, the fear of being alone, the fear of financial loss, the fear of illness, or any other fear, I must remember, Satan capitalizes on fears.

To fear is normal, but how I handle my fears is a matter of life and death—to my physical, spiritual, and emotional health. At times, my fears send me into panic. Other times, they sap my strength and motivation. At other times, they cause my tears to surge and my heart to hammer. Sometimes my fears create thoughts that race down the wild road of imaginations. Satan sends these fears into my heart at the most unexpected times. How do I maintain focus on the promises and character of God when buffeted by fears? Only by God's grace and in His power!

When a mountain suddenly looms in my pathway, it does no good to stop and try to measure it or calculate how I am going to climb it. Rather than focus on the mountain, I must focus on the One who created the mountain. I must focus on His power and His leadership.

When I feel panic, it is time to redirect my thoughts. I must think on God's goodness and faithfulness in the past and pray for His peace. Sitting still and meditating on a comforting verse distracts my fearful mind and calms it. God has given us many verses about not fearing. Often I find a "fear not" verse that gives me strength and post it on an index card where I can read it numerous times throughout the day.

When my strength and motivation have disappeared, I force myself to go outside and work in the sunshine—enough of this gloomy mood! Or, if it's raining, I pick up some unfinished project and set to work. Before long, I find I am enjoying what I am doing.

When the tears flow and I feel bad physically, I allow myself to cry for a while, and then I rest. God calms my heart when I am willing to have it calmed.

When my thoughts race wildly, I endeavor to bring them into captivity by reading the Bible or by thinking of other hurting friends. Sometimes I get out a box of cards and write notes of encouragement—from a discouraged heart! What a paradox! Yet, there is no better way to encourage myself than by encouraging someone else.

For all my fears, I must pray against the powers of Satan, for he is the source of fear. I must remind myself this is not a once-and-done process. Satan is not an easy loser. I must remember that fear brings slavery. Trust in God brings freedom.

> When we have exhausted our store of endurance—
> When our strength has failed ere the day is half done—
> When we reach the end of our hoarded resources—
> Our Father's full giving has only begun.
> He giveth and giveth, and giveth again.
>
> —Annie J. Flint

QUESTIONS

1. What are my most powerful fears right now?
2. What fears have I found victory over?
3. What helps me to restore my focus on God's sufficiency when I'm dealing with fear?
4. How do my fears affect my emotions? Affect me spiritually? Affect me physically?

Compartments

He is the Rock, his work is perfect: for all his ways are judgment: a God of truth and without iniquity, just and right is he. Deuteronomy 32:4

This verse lists the attributes of God in a nutshell. Why do I find it so difficult to surrender to such an almighty, awesome God? Why do I question His dealings with me? Why am I slow to accept His perfect will? Why do I find it difficult to rest in His truth? Why do I fear His decisions?

Perhaps my problem lies in the fact that I want to keep some compartments of my heart closed to God. Perhaps I think there are some things that don't matter to God—they are my choice. Perhaps my fears, my lack of trust, or my unbelief is blinding my eyes to God's power, wisdom, and love. Blindness closes my eyes to the selfish, unclean compartments in my heart. What I don't recognize as wrong or inappropriate, I'm not likely to surrender to God for cleansing.

O Lord, I need a heart- and mind-altering vision of you—a vision that dwells within me through every circumstance and trial. It seems I catch that vision for a short time and then it fades into the clouds of life's realities and difficulties. Help me, Lord to live in the reality of your sovereign character and not in the reality of my weak humanity. Help me to not dwell in the reality of earthly tribulations, but in the reality of heavenly promises.

> Such is the sufficient grace of our God! He can untie all knots of the soul, sever all complexes, and break down the beaten paths of habit though they be securely rooted in the deepest levels of consciousness. His is the power when He is given full sway. He rules in the realms to which He is admitted. If we give Him our souls, He keeps them; if we surrender our hearts, He becomes the center of our affections; if we give Him our minds, He fills us with the mind of Christ; if we submit our whole bodies, he accepts them as His temples and uses our members as instruments of righteousness. The miseries of the Christian world are due to compartmental surrenders.
>
> —Mary Welch

Grant me grace to see you more clearly through the grief-darkened windowpane of my soul. Lord, I surrender all my questions, my fears, my efforts to control, my attempts to hide; I surrender my all to you. I want to invite you into every area of my life. I do not want to surrender only certain compartments! You must have it all, or all is lost.

> Today, beneath thy chastening eye,
> I crave alone for peace and rest;
> Submissive in thy hand to lie,
> And feel that it is best.[37]
>
> —John Greenleaf Whittier

QUESTIONS

1. What most often clouds my vision of God's greatness?
2. Do I have any secret, unsurrendered compartments in my life?
3. If grace is the ability to do things God's way, what hinders God's grace from working for me?

My Father's Way

This is my comfort in my affliction: for thy word hath quickened me. The proud have had me greatly in derision: yet have I not declined from thy law. Psalm 119:50–51

Dr. Bob Overton tells the background of the poem that follows:

> In 1932, my grandfather, A. M. Overton, was a pastor of a church in Mississippi, with a wife and three small children. His wife was pregnant with their fourth child, but when it came time for delivery, there were complications and both she and the baby died. During the funeral service, the preacher officiating the service noticed my grandfather writing something on a piece of paper. After the service the minister asked him about it, and he handed him the paper with a poem he had just written which he titled, "He Maketh No Mistake."[38]

He Maketh No Mistake

My Father's way may twist and turn
My heart may throb and ache
But in my soul I'm glad I know
He maketh no mistake.

My cherished plans may go astray
My hope may fade away,
But still I'll trust my Lord to lead,
For He doth know the way.

Though night be dark and it may seem
That day may never break,
I'll pin my faith, my all on Him;
He maketh no mistake.

There's so much now I cannot see
My eyesight's far too dim,
But come what may, I'll simply trust
And leave it all to Him.

For by and by the mists will lift
And it all plain He'll make
Through all the way, though dark to me;
He made not one mistake.

—A. M. Overton

My Father's way I find in His Word. When I get to the end of myself and my thinking, it is my comfort, my hope, my life. *Thank you, Lord, for your Word, which is my light in the darkness, my reassurance in distress, my expectation in despair.*

God's way is always best;
God's way leads to eternal rest.

QUESTIONS

1. Do I honestly believe God makes no mistakes? Do I feel certain He has made no mistakes in my life?
2. What in my present situation gives me hope right now?
3. If God's way is always best, why must it be so painful?

Gifts of Grief

Be merciful unto me, O God, be merciful unto me: for my soul trusteth in thee: yea, in the shadow of thy wings will I make my refuge, until these calamities be overpast. Psalm 57:1

The dark valley will pass. Tears will pass. The pain will pass. The trials will pass. The calamities will pass.

In the shadow of His wings, wrapped in His mercy and love, I can be confident that these difficult days will pass. When I rest under the shadow of the wings of God's mercy, I can endure the present. I can trust and not be afraid. I can move ahead in the darkness because He is by my side.

Though the intensity of grief may have passed, there are some permanent signatures of grief I will always have to deal with. However, getting through the valley productively is, in part, dependent on my focus.

In time, I have begun to recognize the gifts of grief. When I first saw the phrase, "gifts of grief," I exclaimed, "What can possibly be gifts of grief?"

Grief has brought me pain, emotional upheaval, physical ailments, feelings of uncertainty about everything, disorientation, and loneliness. Grief brings with it plenty of negative results.

But when I stop and analyze what has happened and is happening to me through grief, I have to draw some other conclusions. Truly, my grief experiences have not been all bad. Grief has indeed left me with some priceless gifts. Contact with other grieving people has forged some unique relationships. Grief has given me a more compassionate heart—a gift I really needed. I find myself reaching out to other hurting hearts. I feel more care and compassion for others. Grief has opened my eyes and drawn my mind to my inner needs, my humanity, my finiteness, my mortality. I will not live on this earth forever; heaven is my home. Grief has given me three healthy, sin-free, temptation-free beloved ones who wait joyfully for me. Grief shows that I have loved and been loved.

Grief is teaching me the greatness of God's ways and the smallness of mine. It is teaching me the rightness of God's ways and the faultiness of mine. It is teaching me the love and mercy of God's character and the imperfection of mine. Grief is teaching me to depend on God, His plan and His purpose. It is showing me the folly of depending on my own strength.

QUESTIONS

1. In what areas have I learned to trust God more?
2. Do I recognize any gifts of grief? What are they?
3. How has my understanding of God grown through this trial?

The Mind of Christ

For who hath known the mind of the Lord, that he may instruct him? But we have the mind of Christ. 1 Corinthians 2:16

I do not know the mind of the Lord! I have not the wisdom to instruct Him! So why do I challenge Him and question what He brings into my life?

- The mind of Christ is all-knowing, all-wise, and all-powerful.
- The mind of Christ knows the truth. His life lives the truth. His tongue speaks the truth.
- The mind of Christ loves the good. He continually does good to the hurting and troubled. He always speaks what is good to the searching heart.
- The mind of Christ chooses the right. He daily lives the right. His whole character is right. His whole mind and being is absorbed with His love, mercy, and forgiveness for mankind. He is all righteousness.

How can I have the mind of Christ while facing trials? The mind of Christ is all truth, all good, all righteous, all-loving, all-knowing—mine is not!

I must acquire a knowledge of Christ's mind through His words, His miracles, His conduct, and His sufferings. I must know Him personally. Having the mind of Christ is not a once-and-done deal. It's a daily growing process.

I must receive by faith His truth, His righteousness, His redemption. I must become like Him in love and forgiveness. I must choose to do His will and spread His truth to all mankind.

"The natural man" knows not God, and "receiveth not the things of the Spirit of God" (1 Corinthians 2:14). In science, art, government, and in all sorts of intellectual ventures, the natural man has made great advances and marvelous achievements. But all of this has brought him no nearer to the mind of Christ.

How do I apply all this to all the pain and the unknowns in my life? I must determine not to carry the load of the unknown. There are some battles we do not need to fight! Although it runs contrary to our natural minds, sometimes we just need to stand still in confident faith and wait for the salvation of the Lord. Israel first had to stand still and wait, then move forward in faith.

The fearful Israelites found their way to safety through the Red Sea, the last place one would expect to find safety. "And the children of Israel went into the midst of the sea upon the dry ground: and the waters were a wall unto them on their right hand, and on their left" (Exodus 14:22). Their Egyptian enemies found their defeat in the Red Sea. "And the waters returned, and covered the chariots, and the horsemen, and all the host of Pharaoh that came into the sea after them; there remained not so much as one of them" (Exodus 14:28).

I must commit my pain and sorrow to you, Lord. I must listen to your Holy Spirit and allow you to show me when to stand still and see your salvation and when to move ahead. With the mind of Christ, I will walk out of the dark valley into the sunshine victoriously. I will touch other lives with your love. I will thank you for the trial and affliction.

God is good, God is love, and God is truth; He cannot be otherwise.

QUESTIONS

1. What do I know about the mind of Christ?
2. What am I doing to grow in the mind of Christ?
3. How do I know whether or not I have the mind of Christ?

God's Backward Economy

What am I learning about God and myself while living in the upside-down, inside-out, backward economy of God's structure?

- I find strength by acknowledging my weakness. "Therefore I take pleasure in infirmities, in reproaches, in necessities, in persecutions, in distresses for Christ's sake: for when I am weak, then am I strong" (2 Corinthians 12:10).
- I must lose to save. "For whosoever will save his life shall lose it: but whosoever will lose his life for my sake, the same shall save it" (Luke 9:24).
- I must die to live and produce fruit. "Verily, verily, I say unto you, Except a corn of wheat fall into the ground and die, it abideth alone: but if it die, it bringeth forth much fruit" (John 12:24).
- The "foolishness" of God brings me supreme wisdom. "But God hath chosen the foolish things of the world to confound the wise; and God hath chosen the weak things of the world to confound the things which are mighty" (1 Corinthians 1:27).
- When I humble myself, God exalts me. "For whosoever exalteth himself shall be abased; and he that humbleth himself shall be exalted" (Luke 14:11).
- In Christ, I exchange the old for the new. "Therefore if any man be in Christ, he is a new creature: old things are passed away; behold, all things are become new" (2 Corinthians 5:17).
- I give away to increase. "There is that scattereth, and yet increaseth; and there is that withholdeth more than is meet, but it tendeth to poverty" (Proverbs 11:24).
- When I kill the deeds of the flesh, I live. "For if ye live after the flesh, ye shall die: but if ye through the Spirit do mortify the deeds of the body, ye shall live" (Romans 8:13).
- I surrender to become free. "But God be thanked, that ye were the servants of sin, but ye have obeyed from the heart that form of doctrine which was delivered you. Being then made free from sin, ye became the servants of righteousness" (Romans 6:17–18).

- While my body is dying, my spirit is being transformed to life eternal. "For which cause we faint not; but though our outward man perish, yet the inward man is renewed day by day" (2 Corinthians 4:16).

God's upside down economy works wonders in the surrendered heart. To my human way of thinking, it all seems backward. It takes a renewed mind to agree with God's economy.

QUESTIONS

1. Have I experienced God's backward workings in my life?
2. How have I died to live? What have I lost to find?
3. What have I learned through my tribulation and through God's backward working?
4. Am I ready to move on, finding a new normal and remembering I am a different person who is loved and maintained by God's mercy?

Fear the Lord

O fear the LORD, ye his saints: for there is no want to them that fear him. Psalm 34:9

Where are the desires of my heart? To what or to whom have I surrendered my heart? To whom have I sacrificed my will? At times the answers to these questions are obscured by the dark clouds of fear.

Fear of losing . . .

Fear of what will happen to . . .

Fear of how we as a family will deal with . . .

Fear of what others think of . . .

Fear of total surrender to God!

Monsters of fear stalk through my thoughts, blocking out God's promises in the Scriptures.

- "Fear thou not; for I am with thee: be not dismayed; for I am thy God" (Isaiah 41:10).
- "Blessed is the man that feareth the LORD" (Psalm 112:1).
- "I will fear no evil: for thou art with me" (Psalm 23:4).
- "The fear of the LORD is a fountain of life" (Proverbs 14:27).
- "The LORD is my light and my salvation; whom shall I fear? the LORD is the strength of my life; of whom shall I be afraid?" (Psalm 27:1).

The fears leave for a time, but then return to haunt me. Satan schemes to take away my peace and trust. Again, I must examine myself. Are the desires of my heart surrendered to God's will? Have I sacrificed my will to God's plan? Am I totally surrendered to Him? Someone said, "We will fear that which we surrender our hearts to. Our hearts will always be with our sacrifice." Perfect love casts out fear. *O Lord, increase my love.*

Satan uses the dark places of silence and secrets to destroy a Christian's peace and relationship with God. When my heart is troubled and pained, I must tell Jesus my dark, secret thoughts and feelings. Truly, nothing is secret to Him.

O God, keep my wandering mind stayed on you! Enlighten my understanding of your power, your love, your plan, your ways, your timetable, your purpose. Help me to surrender my doubts to you and to sacrifice my heart on your altar of love. I choose to live in your fear and to know no want. I choose to hand over to you the weight of the unknown and the burden of what has not yet happened.

When I fear God, all other fears fade. Satan loses his control over my mind. The Lord's power enables me to overcome.

Stop telling God how big your storm is.
Instead tell your storm how big your God is!

QUESTIONS

1. What are my present, persistent fears?
2. Do I believe God is bigger than all my fears, that He is stronger than all my doubts? (See the list of God's attributes on page 291, Appendix A.)
3. Does what I believe about God affect how I think about my fears? In what ways?
4. How am I actively fighting my fears?
5. How does the fear of God help diminish my fear of man and circumstances? Are these two different kinds of fear?

No Comparisons

For we dare not make ourselves of the number, or compare ourselves with some that commend themselves: but they measuring themselves by themselves, and comparing themselves among themselves, are not wise. 2 Corinthians 10:12

"Well, everyone has dark valleys and hard times." How many times must I hear that statement? My pain-filled eyes look unseeingly at the speaker, and my subconscious mind begins churning. *She hasn't had any dark valleys compared to what I've gone through. It seems the sun always shines on that family. She thinks she's had it hard, but she doesn't really know what heartache is. She has never had a loss as great as mine. She doesn't know what trouble is.*

Have you had similar experiences? After many such occurrences, God's Spirit has reminded me that I am not wise when I compare myself with others. What measuring stick do they use to measure my grief? What measuring stick do I use to measure their problems? Does God really intend for us to compare our own troubles with someone else's?

I suppose I will never know until I get to heaven—and then it won't matter anymore—why some people have so many trials and dark valleys while others have so few. Really, the question is not how many or how few valleys I have gone through. Neither is the question how dark and difficult the valleys are. The real issue is: How did I go through my valley experience? How did I respond to my trials? Did I overcome and grow through the difficult times, or did the dark times overcome me? Did I merely survive my tribulations or was I more than a conqueror?

God's strong, steadfast saints are not grown in flowerbeds,
but on the rugged mountain heights of trial and suffering.
—author unknown

QUESTIONS

1. Have I ever compared my situation or loss with that of someone else? What do I feel were the advantages or disadvantages of making such a comparison?

2. Why does God say it is not wise to compare myself with someone else?
3. Do I know anyone whose tribulation seems to be much greater than mine? What are my feelings toward that person and that situation?
4. Do I ever feel like God is picking on me?
5. What do I know about God and about this trial I am going through? (Refer to "Who Is God?" page 291 , Appendix A.)

Punishing or Perfecting?

Have mercy upon me, O LORD; for I am weak: O LORD, heal me; for my bones are vexed. Psalm 6:2

This verse is the moan of a saint for the mercy of his God. Old Testament saints regarded their afflictions as evidence of God's anger and displeasure with them. New Testament saints regard their afflictions as evidence of God's love and part of their Father's gracious training according to their need—part of "all things working together for good" (Romans 8:28).

How do I regard my affliction? Do I long to have it quickly removed or am I anxious to learn what God is teaching me?

O Lord, my soul is living in the deep darkness of night. I feel so alone in this dreariness and depression. A huge black cloud covers me. The ghosts of fear, anger, guilt, and loneliness hammer at my heart and pound in my head. This sorrow is too much for me. There are no answers to my questions. There are no rational reasons for my pain. I grope in the dark shadows for purpose and desire in living. The despair is almost overwhelming. The pain and distress in my body and mind consume me.

In the darkness I cry out for God's mercy. I need to feel His nearness. I hear Him whisper, ***I am with you.*** A faint light appears on the horizon. A glimmer of light creeps ever so slowly into the darkness. Morning comes after the long, dark night. The morning light dispels the shadows as I choose to live in the reality of God's love and light.

God has heard my cry. Dawn brightens, bringing hope, reassurance, and peace. God's mercy and grace are a salve of comfort for my broken heart, throbbing head, and aching body. His understanding and forgiveness drive the ghosts away. His medicine of hope affirms that I can go on. In compassion, He lifts me from the chasm of despair. God's very presence is health to my body and strength to my soul.

I have great reason to praise the Lord of my salvation because "He brought me up also out of an horrible pit, out of the miry clay, and set my feet upon a rock, and established my goings. And he hath put a new song in my mouth, even praise unto our God: many shall see it, and fear, and shall trust in the LORD" (Psalm 40:2–3).

QUESTIONS

1. When I feel depressed, what are the contributing factors? Do I feel God is punishing me or perfecting me?
2. How do I fight discouragement?
3. How do I regard my afflictions and trials? By accepting? Blaming? Denying?
4. For what can I praise God in my situation?

Murmuring

Neither let us tempt Christ, as some of them also tempted, and were destroyed of serpents. Neither murmur ye, as some of them also murmured, and were destroyed of the destroyer. Now all these things happened unto them for ensamples: and they are written for our admonition, upon whom the ends of the world are come. Wherefore let him that thinketh he standeth take heed lest he fall. 1 Corinthians 10:9–12

In the wilderness the Israelites murmured against God many times. How they must have tried God's patience! At one point, He was ready to destroy them all, but because of Moses' prayer for the people and concern for protecting God's honor, He chose to save these murmuring people.

- They murmured about the manna God provided.
- They murmured because they wanted flesh to eat.
- They murmured because they did not have water to drink.
- They murmured against the authority of Moses.
- They murmured about the spies' report from Canaan.

Their gracious and forbearing Ruler and Leader finally exclaimed, "Forty years long was I grieved with this generation!" (Psalm 95:10).

In these verses from 1 Corinthians we are warned, "Neither murmur ye!" How often have my prayers been a murmur?

Some murmur, when their sky is clear
And wholly bright to view,
If one small speck of dark appear
In their great heaven of blue;

And some with thankful love are filled
If but one streak of light,
One ray of God's good mercy, gild
The darkness of their night.

In palaces are hearts that ask,
In discontent and pride,
Why life is such a dreary task,
And all things good denied?

And hearts in poorest huts admire
How love has in their aid
(Love that never seems to tire)
Such rich provision made.
—Trench

Lord, help me focus on the streak of light in today's dark sky—remembering this trial, too, will pass. Help me to be aware and thankful when my life's sky becomes brighter. Please help me to choose the spirit of contentment that is "great gain" (1 Timothy 6:6).

When God puts a burden upon you, He puts His own arm underneath.

QUESTIONS

1. What was the Israelites' root problem when they murmured? What is my problem when I murmur?
2. What am I doing to grow in the spirit of contentment?
3. Do I feel I deserve special treatment from God? Why?
4. Is God grieved about something in my life or attitude?

The Carnal Mind

For to be carnally minded is death; but to be spiritually minded is life and peace. Because the carnal mind is enmity against God: for it is not subject to the law of God, neither indeed can be. Romans 8:6-7

Lord, it seems I have an infection of human nature working to make my mind and body sick. "The carnal mind is enmity against God." My human reasoning is making me depressed and confused.

I have looked at my daughter's death from every angle I could possibly imagine. If only I would have had more faith, if only I would have fasted and prayed all night for her, if I would have taught her better how to deal with stress, if only we had chosen a better treatment plan for her, if only she would have taken everything I made for her, if only she would have gone to the doctor sooner . . .

Lord, such a chain of carnal thoughts goes on and on, yet always comes to the same dead end. At times I am angry, and always I am powerless to change what happened to my daughter. My human thinking makes no sense out of God's thinking and plans.

It is said that the "flesh" equally with the "spirit" has its "mind" i.e. its purpose, its aspiration; an activity headed toward a goal.[39] *So, what is the goal of the "mind of the flesh" but to draw my soul away from you, God? "To be carnally minded is death." This is frightening.*

"To be spiritually minded is life and peace." That is where I want to be. Lord, help me to get out of this dreadful self-help mode of thinking! Help me to fling myself helplessly into your arms. Only when I become helpless will I trust you implicitly. Help me proclaim with Job, "Though he slay me, yet will I trust in him" (Job 13:15). *This must be the commitment of my heart. I fall powerless before your mercy and faithfulness. I make a conscious choice to allow you to restore unto me your spirit of peace. Cast out my human carnal reasoning and help me to accept your plan.*

Giving up my will, my way of reasoning, my thwarted wishes, I choose to rest in your plan, Lord. Even though what has happened makes no sense to me now, I trust you to work all things out for the good of everyone involved.

This pain is not just about me. It is about a husband without a wife. It is about five motherless children, five children who still need guidance and training. O Lord, we need the mind of Christ that we might deal wisely with our adversities. We need the mind of submission, the mind of compassion, the mind of love and servitude.

QUESTIONS

God allows loss and adversity for several reasons, including the following:

1. To expose my frailty and sinfulness. In what ways do I feel exposed?
2. To strengthen my faith and to comfort me so I can comfort others. In what ways has my faith been strengthened? How am I comforting others?
3. To purify me. In what ways has my life been purified?
4. To develop a stronger relationship with me. How has my relationship with God become stronger?
5. To prove Himself faithful on my behalf. How has God proved Himself faithful?

A Bouquet

Remember the word unto thy servant, upon which thou hast caused me to hope. This is my comfort in my affliction: for thy word hath quickened me. Psalm 119:49-50

He only had a bouquet—a beautiful bouquet of flowers—flowers he was likely taking home to his wife. Perhaps it was their anniversary, or maybe her birthday, or perhaps it was simply a token of love. Suddenly I choked up and found myself fighting tears. Why would a kind, thoughtful deed cause an avalanche of painful emotions?

Oh, yes, I knew. I have been through similar painful scenarios many times. I have watched a man opening the door for his wife. I have watched a mother shopping with her daughter. I have watched an old person puffing on a cigarette—my daughters and husband never smoked, yet they died young. The pink ribbon that symbolizes fighting cancer makes me angry. Each scene brings with it a different barrage of emotions.

Memories threatened to flood out my senses. My husband used to bring me flowers for our anniversary. My husband used to bring me flowers for my birthday. My husband used to give me flowers just because he knew I loved flowers. Sometimes he would go out to my flower garden and bring in a beautiful rose.

A man with a bouquet—such a lovely sight, yet I am overcome with feelings of frustration, feelings of aloneness, feelings of not being loved or cared for.

A man with a bouquet brings tears. I cried all the way home from the store. Just because I am no longer young does not mean that my heart does not hurt from lack of love. Just because I am not young does not mean that I feel the depth of pain any less. Just because I am no longer young does not mean that I no longer have dreams of a fulfilling life.

A man with a bouquet means there is a woman somewhere who is thought of tenderly. There is a woman somewhere whose heart will be gladdened because someone cares for her and remembers her.

Lord, a man with a bouquet reminds me that you still are growing flowers for me to enjoy—flowers in my garden and flowers in your Word. Your Word gives me hope when I feel unloved. Your Word gives me comfort when I feel lonely. Your Word makes me alive when I feel there is nothing left to live for. Whatever scenario and whatever emotions, I have to bring it all to you, Lord. I am not capable of dealing with such situations alone. Help me to not wallow in self-pity, because it will dehydrate me of all joy.

QUESTIONS

1. What are some painful scenarios I have faced? What emotions did I need to deal with and how did I cope with them?
2. How does God help me when I am having an emotional struggle?

Where Is God's Loving-Kindness?

Whoso is wise, and will observe these things, even they shall understand the lovingkindness of the LORD. Psalm 107:43

Do I stumble over the severity of God's dealings with me or with those I love? Do I question how a God of love can allow such misery and pain on earth? Do I fail to remember that God's thoughts are higher than my thoughts? Do I limit God to earthly time, space, and knowledge?

This psalm talks about great troubles and God's gracious deliverance. However, my life experiences have made me feel like often there is no deliverance. The weary wanderer sinks down on the sand and dies. The criminal perishes in his dungeon. The man stricken with disease passes through the gates of death. The storm-tossed ship goes down with all its passengers and crew. From my human vantage point, the saying seems to ring true: "Deliverances are the exception, not the rule."[40]

We find it difficult to see His loving-kindness in leaving children motherless or fatherless, in leaving mothers childless, in leaving widows and widowers, in leaving people helpless or senseless, in leaving people homeless and jobless, in leaving people starving and cold. These harsh realities are the cruel consequences of sin.

Where is the loving-kindness of God when life gets tough? Where is God's goodness when terrible troubles threaten to crush my faith? Where is God when all feels hopeless? Who am I to question God's wisdom? Who am I to rebel at His counsels?

I look at traumatic events from a perepective of limited time and space, and with imperfect human understanding. God knows no limit of time, space, or understanding. I must quietly wait to see the loving-kindness of God. Often it is only revealed when His work is completed. Many times I may not see the end of His plan, but I must trust that His loving-kindness will be accomplished, someday, some way, sometime. Oh, how I need the mind of Christ!

One way I see the loving-kindness of the Lord at work in my life is His bringing my heart and will into harmony with His. This is His most loving and blessed gift to His child—a heart that always says to God, "Thy will be done." From this place of total surrender, I find courage to cling to the unshakable goodness of God, regardless of the injustice I see around me. Help me, Lord, to trust that your loving-kindness is at work even when I fail to see or feel it! Help me to not expect heavenly perfection here on earth.

QUESTIONS

1. In what ways have I seen the loving-kindness of God during my trial?
2. What things during my trial have caused me to question the loving-kindness of God?
3. What are some ways I can show the loving-kindness of God to other hurting hearts?

But We Trusted

But we trusted that it had been he which should have redeemed Israel: and beside all this, to day is the third day since these things were done. Luke 24:21

How often I find myself feeling depressed and dejected because of shattered expectations! How often I am just like the bewildered men on the way to Emmaus. "But we trusted"—we who were His friends and followers thought we had found in Him the Redeemer of Israel, the Messiah, the King. We thought things were going to turn out differently. Instead, a shameful cross stripped all our hopes away.

Indeed, "Besides all this"—all our crushed expectations—"today is the third day since these things happened!"

The third day! The third week! The third month! The third year and still He has not done what I expected! Why does God not come to my aid? Does He not care that I am waiting on Him?

Was it Jesus' fault that these two men were feeling dejected and stressed? No! These men had misconceived ideas of Jesus' plan, and their misguided expectations gave birth to disappointment and delusion. All the while, Jesus was accomplishing His plan perfectly.

Whenever I feel dejected and stressed, I can be sure it is not God's fault. The blame lies in my messed up expectations. The fault lies in my purpose in prayer. I am demanding that God work according to my vision and plan rather than His.

The men on the road to Emmaus wanted Jesus to be their nation's king and deliverer from the Romans, while Christ's design was to offer redemption and participation in a heavenly kingdom to all of humanity. Jesus' plan was entirely different from their expectations.

By God's grace, I will not sit down on a rocking chair and wait to see how God is going to work out my expectations. Instead, I will get up on my feet and proceed through each day, faithfully doing the mundane while looking for ways to bless others. One day at a time, one task at a time, one prayer at a time, I can accomplish His purpose for my life. By yielding my expectations to God, I free Him to work His plan in me.

QUESTIONS

1. How do I react to disappointments?
2. What crushed expectation am I dealing with right now?
3. What character qualities do I need so that I can accept crushed expectations calmly?
4. Are there disappointments in my past that I have not acknowledged?
5. Do I habitually bury hurts and disappointments, pretend they are not there, or harp on them? Do I discuss them with a friend who can help me work through them? Do I take my hurts to the Lord and ask Him to help me?

The Eye of the Lord

Behold, the eye of the LORD is upon them that fear him, upon them that hope in his mercy. Let thy mercy, O LORD, be upon us, according as we hope in thee. Psalm 33:18, 22

If I want the eye of the Lord to be upon me, I must . . .
fear Him,
hope in His mercy,
wait on His direction,
and trust in His holy name.

His eye will be upon me . . .
to deliver and direct me,
to help me,
to strengthen me,
to give me courage,
to protect me,
to comfort me.

According to my hope—my trusting confidence—even so will His mercy and care be to me. My heart shall rejoice in His care.

I will bear the scars of my losses throughout my life. Until I die, my losses will continue to influence my thinking and my responses, shaping who I am. Emptiness, sorrow, and longing are a part of my life. My life is forever changed. I can identify with the writer who said that the pain of his loss is woven into the fabric of his being.[41] Like him, I feel that the pain I have experienced is a part of who I have become.

Not all the good, nor all the growth that I have received as the result of my losses can ever make the losses good in themselves. Nevertheless, courage, hope, and anticipation are also a part of my life.

Help me, Lord, to face the darkness of my losses while learning to live in and share the light of your mercy and grace.

QUESTIONS

1. What does it mean to me to have the eye of the Lord upon me?
2. What are some experiences that are woven into the fabric of my being?
3. God never fails, but my faulty thinking may make it appear that He did. Am I rejoicing in God's care, or do I feel He has failed me in some way?

Faith as a Mustard Seed

And when he was come into the house, the blind men came to him: and Jesus saith unto them, Believe ye that I am able to do this? They said unto him, Yea, Lord. Then touched he their eyes, saying, According to your faith be it unto you. Matthew 9:28–29

When we are going through a severe trial or things seem to be turning out wrong, do we blame ourselves for not having enough faith? Or when we lose a loved one, do we feel that perhaps if we would have had enough faith he would have lived? We can have these secret doubts when we lose our job, our health, or our home, wondering if it happened because of our lack of faith. Do we think God is frowning down on us, sending these things because our faith is not great enough? Do we think He enjoys seeing us, His children, anxious or guilty concerning our faith? No, God loves us and desires that we grow in faith.

Jesus talked about people's faith numerous times. He said to the blind men, "According to your faith be it unto you" (Matthew 9:29). This verse is frightening and heart searching. Does my lack of faith hinder God from accomplishing His work? In Matthew 6:30, Jesus comments on little faith: "Wherefore, if God so clothe the grass of the field, which to day is, and to morrow is cast into the oven, shall he not much more clothe you, O ye of little faith?"

Matthew 8:26 recounts His rebuke to His disciples for their lack of faith: "He saith unto them, Why are ye fearful, O ye of little faith? Then he arose, and rebuked the winds and the sea; and there was a great calm."

Jesus found great faith in the centurion who asked Jesus to heal his servant. "And [Jesus] turned him about, and said unto the people that followed him, I say unto you, I have not found so great faith, no, not in Israel" (Luke 7:9).

Jesus leaves us this challenge: "I say unto you, If ye have faith as a grain of mustard seed, ye shall say unto this mountain, Remove hence to yonder place; and it shall remove; and nothing shall be impossible unto you" (Matthew 17:20).

Jesus discerned each person's faith, and He worked according to that faith. Sometimes He worked in spite of the person's little faith. The words and works of Jesus were always meant to encourage the growth of faith, helping people to see the foolishness of their lack of faith.

Is faith about performance or is it about my relationship with God? My faith is about my relationship with God and my performance of His will—not just at church on Sundays, but in everyday life, in every area of life. Faith is not a button to push to get God to operate the way I think He should. Faith is a heartstring of love and trust from my heart to God's, a connection that grows stronger as my relationship with God grows closer.

Why doesn't my faith always accomplish what I think it should? Because I do not know the mind of God. I cannot understand His thoughts. His ways are higher than mine; therefore, He and I do not always come to the same conclusion. As my knowledge of God grows and my experience of His faithfulness deepens, I will find it easier to lean on Him in faith that triumphs over adversity.

Never focus on your weak faith; focus on God's strength.

QUESTIONS

1. "According to your faith be it unto you" (Matthew 9:29). Does that mean if I have faith, my prayers will be answered the way I want them to be answered? Why or why not?
2. Is my faith about performance or relationship?
3. Do I feel condemnation about my lack of faith in any area of my life? How should I deal with that?
4. When God does not answer my prayer the way I expect, how do I respond?
5. What did the man say in Mark 9:24? Has this ever been my prayer?

Focus

Set your affection on things above, not on things on the earth. Colossians 3:2

This verse speaks about living a focused life. On what or on whom am I focused? How important is it to be focused? What is my mind set on? As the saying goes, "Tell me what a man thinks, and I can tell you what he is." What is the object of my thought and endeavor?

Would we choose a brain surgeon who is known for telling college-day stories during surgery? How important is focus when a traveler drives through New York City at rush hour? How much focus does a scientist need to look through a telescope or microscope? His mind, eye, and the instrument must be focused concurrently if he wishes to discover anything.

Success comes to those who are focused on good and right ambitions. Haphazard living results in confusion and disappointment. Those who are not focused or who are focused on the wrong things suffer painful consequences such as addictions, trouble, and jail.

Christ's formula for a successful life is focus: "Set your affection on things above." His remedy for those suffering in trials and heartaches is to focus on His almighty goodness and compassion. His answer for the valley of the shadow of death is to focus on His strength, hope, and eternal life.

My focus and priorities need adjusting many times. Situations, trials, and hardships tend to change my sense of direction. My health needs, family needs, and church needs often modify my focus. I must examine my priorities, pray, and ask God's help and direction in making necessary changes. When my affection is set on things above, my mind will be filled with heavenly thoughts and trusting hope. What a goal to strive for!

When the path ahead points toward darkness, sorrow, loss, or death, it is difficult to focus on things above. Yet, when my affection is set on heavenly things, I can see beauty through tears. I can see God's love through my fears. I can feel God's empathy through pain. *O Lord, help me keep my focus on you!*

> Oh, who, in such a world as this,
> Could bear his lot of pain,
> Did not one radiant hope of bliss
> Unclouded yet remain?

That hope the Sovereign Lord has given,
Who reigns above the skies;
Hope that unites the soul to heaven
By faith's endearing ties.

—author unknown

QUESTIONS

1. On what is my affection set? What is the most important thing in my life?
2. How does my focus affect my daily living?
3. How can I begin to change my focus and priorities?

Stay Put

O keep my soul, and deliver me: let me not be ashamed; for I put my trust in thee. Psalm 25:20

When I put a book on the shelf, I put it in the place where it belongs.
When I put a plate on the table, I put it there for a purpose and need.
When I put flowers on a stand, I put them there to create an atmosphere of beauty.
When I put eggs in a pot on the stove, I put them there to make them edible.
When I put my trust in the Lord, I put my trust where it belongs.
When I put my trust in the Lord, I put it there with purpose and need.
When I put my trust in the Lord, I put it there to create an atmosphere of peace and confidence.
When I put my trust in the Lord, I put it there to keep my life livable and worthwhile.

To *put* something is to deliberately place with a purpose. This is exactly what I must do with my trust. I must deliberately place my trust in my unchanging, ever reliable, always loving, never failing God.

When sunny day follows sunny day and life flows as a babbling brook, I do not stop to examine my trust. Too often I operate on presumption. Life is going smoothly, so I presume it will continue that way. My trust in the Lord relaxes when there are no rocks in my path and no mountains to climb.

Then God suddenly drops a trial in my path that awakens and prods my trust! When a boulder abruptly falls on my path, where do I turn for strength to go around it or over it? Where do I go for wisdom and direction to help me through the uncertainties and tests of life? Where do I look for peace and comfort for my aching heart?

Do I have the inner resources and spiritual strength to seek God's help? Or have I been so independent from God, operating in my own strength, that I am oblivious of my need to trust and depend on God?

If I have not been walking the "trust and depend on God" walk, then I must consciously begin cultivating trust until it becomes a habit. I cannot do this without forsaking my proud, independent spirit.

Lord, grant me Paul's spirit of dependence: "Most gladly therefore will I rather glory in my infirmities, that the power of Christ may rest upon me. Therefore I take pleasure in infirmities, in reproaches, in necessities, in persecutions, in distresses for Christ's sake: for when I am weak, then am I strong" (2 Corinthians 12:9–10).

Never operate on presumption. Adjust your trust!

QUESTIONS

1. What do I need to do to put my trust in God?
2. How does trust in God affect my life, my joy, my stress?
3. How have my problems tried and increased my faith?
4. What are some things I presume about God when life is going smoothly?
5. When a "bomb" suddenly drops in my life, how do I react? Do I panic or pray? Do I fight or yield? Do I freeze or face it?

Song in the Night

But none saith, Where is God my maker, who giveth songs in the night? Job 35:10
I call to remembrance my song in the night: I commune
with mine own heart: and my spirit made diligent search. Psalm 77:6
Ye shall have a song, as in the night when a holy solemnity is kept. Isaiah 30:29

What do I do when I realize my situation is getting worse? When the body is deteriorating and the monster of disease is raging? When the spirit is growing more rebellious? When the purse is getting emptier? When the storm of tribulation is growing stronger, and I feel more and more out of control?

I felt this way as I watched my daughter's health deteriorate. Her spirit was growing stronger while her body was growing weaker. I cried out, *O Lord! There is nothing more I can do. It will take a miracle from you. And what if you choose to not do that miracle? Lord, help me to surrender to your will. Oh, I thank you for the song in the night!*

It was one of those bad nights, a night when I woke up every hour or hour and a half. Every time I awoke, these words with their music were echoing clearly through my mind: "Thy ways are infinitely great and sometimes hard to understand." Each time I awakened with those words in my head, I pondered, "Where are those words from?" Finally, in the morning I determined the words were from the song, "I Saw a Wounded Robin." It was a song I did not know well, but God had brought the words to me again and again throughout the night: "Thy ways are infinitely great and sometimes hard to understand."

When I shared with my daughter Sonya about my song in the night, she said, "That must have been a great encouragement to you."

I swallowed hard and nodded, "I guess so." I did not want to tell her the questions I had at the moment. In my mind a battle raged. Would I experience His ways infinitely great in His healing her? Or was this experience going to be hard to understand? Inwardly I cried, *Help me, Lord, to focus on your greatness in this hard-to-understand trial!*

Indeed, in retrospect, I have experienced both aspects of God's ways in this trial. Truly, "[His] ways are infinitely great and sometimes hard to understand."

Thank you, Lord, for the song in the night!

QUESTIONS

1. In what ways is my situation growing worse?
2. When things get worse, what do I tend to do—reach out to God, try harder, or find people to talk to?
3. Are there any special ways in which God has reached out to me during this trial?
4. In what area do I find it difficult to submit to God?

A Lesson in the Snow

On the left hand, where he doth work, but I cannot behold him: he hideth himself on the right hand, that I cannot see him: but he knoweth the way that I take: when he hath tried me,I shall come forth as gold. Job 23:9–10

As I was driving over to my daughter's house in a borrowed car on strange roads, I suddenly found my car sitting astride a snowdrift. An early spring snowstorm with wild winds had started the day before. I had just slowed down to drive through ruts of slush and mud when suddenly the road went white before me, giving no indication of the depth of the drift. The car came to a crunching halt with snow piled high around it. Spring, new life, and hope seemed far away. Just as my car was stranded, I felt stranded emotionally in my present experience—I could not move forward or backward. I was stuck in pain and frustration, wondering where God would take me next. Thankfully, I had a cell phone, so help was only a call away. Soon my son-in-law and grandson arrived, pushing through high drifts with their pickup. After many maneuverings, they got the truck turned around and fastened a towrope to the little car.

"Just put it in drive and help me," my son-in-law said. "The drifts are too deep for this little car. I'll have to pull you out to the main road."

And pull he did! With his mind and eyes on the snow-drifted road ahead, he gunned his truck through the snow. He had no idea what was going on behind him. It was the wildest ride I have ever had. The little car slid from one side of the road to the other. I fully expected that at any moment the little car would land in the ditch and be dragged along bottom side up! The windshield was covered with muddy snow. *I guess it doesn't matter if I can't see,* I thought. *I have no control over where I'm going anyhow. O God, keep me safe!*

After I arrived safely at my daughter's home, I had time to reflect on my nerve-shattering experience. I realized with thanksgiving that God is not in the same position my son-in-law had been, unaware of what was happening behind him. When I call on God for help, He sometimes answers even before I call. He is aware of all that is going on in my life and in the lives of my loved ones. He knows all about the unfamiliar, snow-covered road. He knows about the blind spots. God does not speed down the road ahead of me, dragging me along. He walks along beside me, holding my hand.

Later, my son-in-law remarked, "That little car was terribly hard to pull."

Ruefully I had to confess, "I had the brakes on sometimes, trying to keep it under control!"

Lord, forgive me when I put the brakes on and make the way ahead more difficult because I am fighting for control. It is so hard to trust when I cannot see the way ahead, yet when I surrender to you I can be confident in your all-seeing, all-powerful care.

QUESTIONS

1. How do I feel and respond when I am not in control?
2. What lessons might God want to teach me by putting me in circumstances over which I have no control?
3. What is the message to me from Job 23:9–10?

The End of My Rope

My times are in thy hand. Be of good courage, and he shall strengthen your heart, all ye that hope in the LORD. Psalm 31:15, 24

Am I speeding through life, running downhill faster and faster until I can no longer keep up with myself and fall flat on my face? Life is more than paying bills, buying frills, and seeking thrills. Is it any wonder that we feel exhausted, irritated, and at the end of our rope when this is our lifestyle?

However, even though I am not buying frills or seeking thrills, yet I often feel at the end of my rope. Trials and dilemmas make my mind and body tense. My bottled up emotions make my brain dull and my spirit tired. I am exhausted, but cannot sleep unless I let go of my rope of self-sufficiency and latch on to God's promises to supply my need.

A change of focus does wonders for intense moments of frustration and hopelessness. A quiet time with God stills my pounding heart and calms my racing, irrational thoughts.

Regardless of my reasons for being at the end of my rope, the problem is basically the same. I must ask myself these questions:

- What is my goal or purpose in life?
- Whom am I living for?
- Whom am I trying to impress, serve, or glorify?
- Whom or what do I trust when my life feels out of control?

When my hope, my goal, and my trust are in the Lord, He supplies strength and courage for all that I face. He holds my times in His hands, and I can rest. He is at the other end of my rope!

Take time to be holy, speak oft with thy Lord;
Abide in Him always, and feed on His Word.
Make friends of God's children, help those who are weak,
Forgetting in nothing His blessing to seek.

Take time to be holy, the world rushes on;
Spend much time in secret, with Jesus alone.
By looking to Jesus, like Him thou shalt be;
Thy friends in thy conduct His likeness shall see.

Take time to be holy, let Him be thy Guide;
And run not before Him, whatever betide.
In joy or in sorrow, still follow the Lord,
And, looking to Jesus, still trust in His Word.

Take time to be holy, be calm in thy soul,
Each thought and each motive beneath His control.
Thus led by His Spirit to fountains of love,
Thou soon shalt be fitted for service above.

—William Longstaff

QUESTIONS

1. Have I been speeding through life? What have I missed along the way?
2. What are the things that bring me to the end of my rope?
3. How am I using the "busy syndrome" or the "do nothing" cop-out as a cover-up?
4. What do I need to change about the way I use my time?

Sufficient

But seek ye first the kingdom of God, and his righteousness; and all these things shall be added unto you. Take therefore no thought for the morrow: for the morrow shall take thought for the things of itself. Sufficient unto the day is the evil thereof. Matthew 6:33–34

Have you ever felt you have had sufficient evil for the day, the month, or the year? Do you feel you have more than your share of hurts?

- Sufficient pain?
- Sufficient trouble?
- Sufficient anxiety?
- Sufficient sorrow?
- Sufficient tears?

God promises sufficient grace! He gives us strength to hold on when the trials come. His grace is enough to carry us through each moment, each day. God understands our humanity, and He only supplies for the present day. If we had a way to store up an extra supply of God's grace, we would not need to depend on God daily. We would just take out some grace whenever we needed it, and soon we would be thinking how well *we* are taking care of our problems.

God wisely supplies only enough for the present day. As the song says, "Yesterday's gone and tomorrow may never come!"[42] He knows I am not strong enough to relive yesterday's trials or think ahead to tomorrow's. Therefore, He says, "Sufficient unto the day." He wants me to live free from anxiety concerning the past or apprehension about the future.

Many years ago, Abraham Lincoln was interviewed concerning his views of the impending Civil War. He replied, "I am much like the old preacher in a crowded coach nearing a swollen river. He had listened in silence to the wearisome expressions of anxiety respecting the perilous fording of the stream until the passengers, somewhat vexed at his seeming indifference, asked his opinion. He replied, 'I make it a practice never to cross a river till I get to it.' "

Well, Lord, that would certainly free me from a lot of anxiety and reduce the number of my sleepless nights! Grant me the wisdom, fortitude, and faith to leave the river crossing until I get there.

Some of your hurts you have cured,
And the sharpest you still have survived;
But what torments of grief you endured
From evils which never arrived!

—Ralph Waldo Emerson

QUESTIONS

1. What are some things that have felt overwhelming to me?
2. Do I feel God has been unjustly hard on me? In what ways?
3. What rivers have I crossed before I got there, causing myself needless pain?
4. Anxiety is the natural result of sudden changes. What are some ways I can reduce my anxiety?

Exhausted Mercies?

Is his mercy clean gone for ever? doth his promise fail for evermore? Hath God forgotten to be gracious? hath he in anger shut up his tender mercies? Selah. Psalm 77:8–9

Is it possible to exhaust God's mercies? No, we can never exhaust them, but doubt can greatly cloud our minds so that we cannot see the goodness of God. When afflictions come from without, and doubts come from within, it is easier to focus on the outward trials than to acknowledge the inward doubts.

When God allows our afflictions—outward circumstances—to become overwhelming, He is saying, "Focus on me, not on your circumstances." "[God] will not suffer you to be tempted above that ye are able" (1 Corinthians 10:13). I become overwhelmed when I allow my thought patterns and circumstances to overshadow what I know about God's character.

The doubts, the fears, and the questions crush my spirit. Where is God? Is He really my God? Does He really care? Will He keep his promises?

In Psalm 77:8–9, David's desperation may have arisen from his concern over his rebellious son from whom he was fleeing. Moreover, while he thought on Absalom's treachery, he likely remembered the prophet Nathan's words of judgment after his great sin with Bathsheba: "Thus saith the LORD, Behold, I will raise up evil against thee out of thine own house" (2 Samuel 12:11). Besides this, David's enemies taunted him, "Where is thy God?" (Psalm 42:10).

The sting of his own sin, his guilt, his son's sin, and the taunting of his enemies was too much! "Is his mercy clean gone for ever?" David cried out.

"O aching, grieving heart, I will remember that no afflictions, doubts, or guilt of sin—nothing is able to make God's mercies fail. Afflictions, doubts, and guilt can cloud my vision of Him, but they cannot change Him. God's character does not change with my changing thoughts and moods. What a blessed fact: 'He abideth faithful' " (2 Timothy 2:13).

"Justice and judgment are the habitation of thy throne: mercy and truth shall go before thy face" (Psalm 89:14). Whatever God does, He does in mercy and truth because this is His character. "O satisfy us early with thy mercy; that we may rejoice and be glad all our days" (Psalm 90:14).

God, help me be satisfied and confident in your mercy!

QUESTIONS

1. Do God's mercies seem "clean gone" to me ?
2. Does it seem like God is angry with me?
3. Am I dealing with guilt, disappointments, people pressure, or anger?
4. What do I need to do to un-cloud my vision of God?

Hope—
A Trusting Confidence

Blessed be the God and Father of our Lord Jesus Christ, which according to his abundant mercy hath begotten us again unto a lively hope by the resurrection of Jesus Christ from the dead, to an inheritance incorruptible, and undefiled, and that fadeth not away, reserved in heaven for you, who are kept by the power of God through faith unto salvation ready to be revealed in the last time. 1 Peter 1:3–5

We often express a wishful desire by saying, "I hope it rains tomorrow," or "I hope this pain goes away soon." Our hope in Christ is much stronger than these kinds of desires. It is more than a wish, it is a trusting confidence! In these verses from 1 Peter, I find my lifeline from this troubled and painful earth to the eternal glories of heaven—a living hope that makes my inheritance sure. What is the inheritance for which I hope?

- This inheritance is incorruptible. Things of earth decay and change, but the heavenly kingdom never changes and "cannot be moved" (Hebrews 12:28).
- This inheritance is undefiled. "There shall in no wise enter into it any thing that defileth" (Revelation 21:27).
- This kingdom "fadeth not away" (1 Peter 1:4). It endures eternally.
- This inheritance includes a mansion reserved for me. "In my Father's house are many mansions: if it were not so, I would have told you. I go to prepare a place for you. And if I go and prepare a place for you, I will come again, and receive you unto myself; that where I am, there ye may be also" (John 14:2–3).

When I live with this hope in view, what does it do for my heart? It expels anxiety, fear, doubt, and melancholy. God has promised a hope that "maketh not ashamed" (Romans 5:5) and "full assurance of hope" (Hebrews 6:11). Hope produces confidence, strength of purpose, and peace. The God of hope is the true and eternal source of our hope, which is founded on His sure promises, His mighty mercy, and His abounding grace.

Because Christ arose from the grave, we have a "lively hope . . . an inheritance incorruptible, and undefiled, and that fadeth not away" (1 Peter 1:3–4).

Because of Christ's unchanging character, we have a hope that is "an anchor of the soul, both sure and stedfast, and which entereth into that within the veil" (Hebrews 6:19).

Because Christ ascended into heaven and sent His Holy Spirit to us, we have hope through the power of the Holy Spirit. "Now the God of hope fill you with all joy and peace in believing, that ye may abound in hope, through the power of the Holy Ghost" (Romans 15:13).

Thank you, God, for the hope of an eternal home and an enduring inheritance. Thank you for a hope that keeps me anchored during the storms of life. Thank you for the hope that brings joy, peace, and assurance to your trusting children.

> O living hope, undying power
> I count on you in life's dark hour.
>
> —author unknown

Hope never looks backward—always forward and upward.

QUESTIONS

1. Why is God called "the God of hope"?
2. How does hope work in my heart? What does it achieve?
3. What am I hoping for in my present situation?
4. What are some things that cause me to feel hopeless?
5. What restores my hope?

Enduring to the End

Behold, we count them happy which endure. Ye have heard of the patience of Job, and have seen the end of the Lord; that the Lord is very pitiful, and of tender mercy. James 5:11

In his questions and his desire for God to be his mediator, Job was impatient. Perhaps the reproofs and accusations of his friends aroused in Job the urge to justify himself. How often do my friends make me feel like I need to defend myself?

Job's triumph lies in the fact that his faith did not fail. He had a deep inward certainty of the character of God even though he could not understand why his life had suddenly gone haywire. He clung to that faith until he saw and experienced the "end of the Lord."

Job was certain that . . .

- God is living.
- God is just.
- God is righteous.
- God would bring him forth as gold.

Job believed God would prove and show His character in His perfect timing. That was patience! That was steadfast endurance in faith and love and loyalty to the Lord.

Job's end view of the Lord was that He is full of pity, compassion, tenderness, and mercy. Despite the horror of Job's trials, he passed the test of trusting God, even though he did not understand the calamities God had permitted.

O God, help me to keep the view of the "end of the Lord"! Your end purpose is of much greater importance than the beginning of the trial or the painful enduring in the middle of it. My desire to end a trial comes much too soon, long before your purpose is accomplished. Help me, Lord, to endure to your end! I must trust your sovereign purpose and move forward in peace.

The strength of a man consists in finding out the way God is going, and going that way too.

—Henry Ward Beecher

QUESTIONS

1. What facts about God help me to endure difficult things?
2. What is the most difficult thing I have had to endure?
3. Am I aware of the direction God is going and am I going that way also?
4. Do I have patience to wait for the "end of the Lord"?

My Calling

Wherefore also we pray always for you, that our God would count you worthy of this calling, and fulfill all the good pleasure of his goodness, and the work of faith with power. 2 Thessalonians 1:11

What is the Christian's calling?

- I am called to be His child. "Behold, what manner of love the Father hath bestowed upon us, that we should be called the sons of God: therefore the world knoweth us not, because it knew him not" (1 John 3:1).
- I am called according to His purpose. "And we know that all things work together for good to them that love God, to them who are the called according to his purpose" (Romans 8:28).
- I have a high calling. "I press toward the mark for the prize of the high calling of God in Christ Jesus" (Philippians 3:14).
- I have a holy calling. "Who hath saved us, and called us with an holy calling, not according to our works, but according to his own purpose and grace, which was given us in Christ Jesus before the world began" (2 Timothy 1:9).
- I have a heavenly calling. "Wherefore, holy brethren, partakers of the heavenly calling, consider the Apostle and High Priest of our profession, Christ Jesus" (Hebrews 3:1).
- I am called to liberty. "For, brethren, ye have been called unto liberty; only use not liberty for an occasion to the flesh, but by love serve one another" (Galatians 5:13).
- I am called to peace. "And let the peace of God rule in your hearts, to the which also ye are called in one body; and be ye thankful" (Colossians 3:15).
- I am called to eternal life. "Fight the good fight of faith, lay hold on eternal life, whereunto thou art also called, and hast professed a good profession before many witnesses" (1 Timothy 6:12).

We do indeed have a high calling, but what about the painful place God has called us to now? Sometimes we wonder if we are just called to pain, suffering, and sorrow. Are we just called to trials, troubles, and losses? Are we worthy of no better calling than that of a widow, a widower, a forsaken wife, a single person, a childless parent?

These callings are painful, but important. Have I accepted my calling gracefully and willingly? It will be evident to those around me if I am finding His grace sufficient and depending on His mercy.

As we read the above verses, we should apply them to our present calling. They apply when life flows smoothly and also when the road gets rough. In spite of the pain and discomfort, we have a high and holy calling.

QUESTIONS

1. God calls His people to many different walks and services. What are some of the callings God has given me?
2. Which of my callings do I find difficult and hard to understand?
3. What will help me to accept the difficult callings in a God-honoring way?
4. How is God shaping me through my difficult calling?

I Can Count on Him

But the Lord is faithful, who shall stablish you, and keep you from evil. 2 Thessalonians 3:3

How do we deal with a person we cannot count on? He never comes at the time he says he will. He does not do anything he tells us he will do. The only thing we can count on is the fact that we cannot count on him. Oh, my! How glad I am that my God is not like that!

This verse says God will ESTABLISH—
hold firm, keep,
approve, sanction,
strengthen, fortify,
settle and bolster His saint

Because He is FAITHFUL—
truthful, believable,
trustworthy, devoted,
dependable, and committed.

He who has begun a good work in me will carry it on to completion. He who intercedes for me in heaven will obtain His requests. He who has given me His Spirit will not withhold His grace. He who is the Lord of all comfort will uphold His trembling saint. He who is the Lord of peace will bestow His peace on my fainting heart. He is faithful. Therefore, I can count on Him.

Humans often are not faithful; even my friends will fail me at times. I cannot always count on them. They will disappoint and hurt me. In turn, I must remember that I have not always been faithful. I have failed; I have caused hurt. However, I have a Friend who never fails because He is faithful and true. His promises are sure; His love is pure; His peace will endure.

He will establish me, keeping me strong and firm. He will guard me from the evil one. Others can have confidence in me when I place my confidence in the Faithful One.

When I try to establish my place in life, my cause, my purpose, I will be a failure. But when I allow my faithful God to "stablish and keep" me from evil, I can be assured of success that glorifies His name.

Success isn't measured by what you achieve,
But by obstacles you overcome.
—Ethan Hawke

QUESTIONS

1. Have I been faithful to God? To my family? To the church? To my friends?
2. Can people count on me keeping my word?
3. How do I know I can count on God keeping His Word?
4. Read 2 Thessalonians 3:3, Hebrews 10:23, and 1 John 1:9. How does God prove Himself faithful?

Rejoicing, Patient, Steadfast

Rejoicing in hope; patient in tribulation; continuing instant in prayer. Romans 12:12

In hope rejoicing; in tribulation patiently enduring; in prayer continuing steadfastly—that is God's desire for us.

If all things were as we wished them to be, we would have nothing to hope for. If there were no trials to bear and no tests to endure, we would have no need of patience. If we never felt a need or heartache, we would have little use for prayer—other than thanksgiving—and likely we would not be thankful. A comfortable, happy, trouble-free life does not generally foster gratitude.

Affliction, trials, and heartache drive us to our knees and press out our life blood to produce these necessary Christian virtues. Tribulation is the divine discipline that forms the image of Christ in us.

Too often I am willing to work for God, but I find it difficult to submit to His will. Being ready to serve is easier than being ready to suffer. I take it as my duty to obey God's commands, but have I found the power to endure life's calamities and weaknesses?

There are seasons of my life when I could almost make it in my own strength, happily and devotedly serving Christ my way. Then comes a time of sickness, of calamity, of great tribulation, or of old age, when suddenly I need to learn another aspect of the Christian life. Then I turn in helplessness to God for grace to go on. In the difficult times I learn that God never fails. I learn to trust Him in ways I never have had to trust before. I learn to rejoice in hope, to be patient in trial, and to persist in prayer.

It is easier to work with diligence and strenuousness
than to endure trial without complaint.
—author unknown

QUESTIONS

1. What hopes am I rejoicing in during this time of tribulation?
2. Am I steadfast or stubborn, steady or shifty, sweet or sour in my submission to God?
3. In what specific ways do I especially need patience during this trial?

Confidence

Cast not away therefore your confidence, which hath great recompense of reward. For ye have need of patience, that, after ye have done the will of God, ye might receive the promise. Hebrews 10:35-36

Does God ever need to give me a pep talk? What are some of the things He might say to me?

Cast not away your confidence, my child. I am with you even in the darkest valley or on the steepest mountain. If you remain in my will, you will receive the full and final enjoyment of the glories, peace, and rest of eternal heaven.

The important point is that you steadfastly persevere in faith and hope. When you do my will readily, patiently, and joyfully, your duty will become your freedom, dignity, and delight. I am sure you find that hard to believe, but just trust me. My Word has never failed you in the past, it does not fail you in the present, and it will not fail you in the future.

Never cast away your confidence—especially not when the way gets rough, for then you need confidence and assurance more than ever.

Then when life smooths out and the way becomes easier, do not forget the confidence you had in me when the way was rough. When the way is smooth and easy, you need that confidence to help keep your focus in a heavenly direction.

Confidence is the root that reaches into the faithful heart of God, and patience is the fruit that rests in the promises of God. Out of confidence grows endurance. You must endure hardness as a good soldier. Afflictions, sorrows, and disappointments require patience. You have need of patience to wait for the recompense of reward. Your inheritance is yet coming, my child.

Hang on, be faithful, keep your confidence, be patient! It will be worth it all!

QUESTIONS

1. What is my confidence level in God? In other people?
2. What might cause me to cast away my confidence in Christ and my relationship with Him?

A Growing Faith

We are bound to thank God always for you, brethren, as it is meet, because that your faith groweth exceedingly, and the charity of every one of you all toward each other aboundeth. 2 Thessalonians 1:3

Growing in faith should be the daily aim and duty of the Christian. When faith grows, the fruits of faith increase. A feeble faith makes a feeble Christian. When the whole head is sick, the whole heart is faint (Isaiah 1:5).

A grieving person has a very sick head and faint heart, but thanks to the Lord, this, too, will pass! The more we immerse our hearts in God's Word, the sooner our heads will begin to clear and our thoughts become discernible and sensible. This process takes time and much of God's mercy and grace.

Faith is always known by its works. What are some signs of growing faith?

- Brighter cheerfulness—Doubts distress me less. Torments of fears weaken me less. I bear my pain more patiently. I learn to trust God more fully.
- Deeper devotion—The more faith I have in God, the closer my relationship with Him. The more I depend on Him, the less I depend on myself.
- Warmer love—Faith works by love (Galatians 5:6). The closer I am to God, the more love I have for Him and the more love and care I have for my fellowmen.
- A new song—Confident faith in the goodness of God expresses itself in joyful song. As I focus on God's attributes, even as I experience them in the midst of my losses, I will be motivated to sing.
- A desire to reach out—Faith in God's power and goodness will compel me to reach out to the hearts and lives of others. The grace of God gives me energy for doing the work of God.

Is there anything we can do to help faith grow? Faith grows by what it feeds on. Faith will not grow simply because we wish it to grow. We must feed our faith through the study of God's Word, the study of God's character, and through prayer. Faith will not grow without cultivation. Faith grows by exercise and by remembering God's past mercies, answers to prayer, and blessings. Memories keep faith alive and growing. We exercise faith by getting out of our comfort zones.

> Faith is the instrument by which I grasp divine strength that is made perfect in my weakness.
>
> —author unknown

QUESTIONS

1. What signs of faith do I see in my life?
2. James Matthew Barrie said, "To have faith is to have wings."[43] What could that mean in my life right now? Do I need wings?
3. How am I feeding my faith?

Footsteps Unknown

But it is good for me to draw near to God: I have put my trust in the Lord GOD, that I may declare all thy works. Psalm 73:28
Thy way is in the sea, and thy path in the great waters, and thy footsteps are not known. Psalm 77:19

Are you befuddled by God's ways? Do they seem mysterious? Are you trying to anticipate His next step? Are you wishing His way would go in a different direction? Are you wishing you could be sure of what's ahead?

The story is told of a father who was sitting in his study one day when he looked up from his book, and saw his little son standing precariously on the window ledge. He was terribly frightened, for the child stood in great danger of falling to the ground and being killed.

The little boy had been anxious to know what his father was doing so many hours each day in his study. So he daringly climbed a ladder until he stood there outside the window, gazing at his father with wide eyes. As he took the child into the room and rebuked him for his folly, the father said, "So have I often tried to climb into the council-chamber of God, to see the why and wherefore He did this and that; and thus have I exposed myself to the peril of falling to my own destruction."[44]

It is good to draw near to God—not perched precariously on the ledge with questioning mind and eyes, but humbly falling at His feet in trusting prayer. When I am at peace with God, I will draw near in faith, faith evidenced by total surrender to God's will. On my knees near to God, I learn not to worry myself in trying to understand the hidden ways of God. When I draw near to God, His light of love melts away the fog and mists, and I find calm even in the midst of uncertainty.

Wondering what God is up to is normal, but let's take care to see God in His rightful place when we question Him. God is never challenged or threatened by our questions. God welcomes our questions, but we should not demand immediate answers. Job asked many questions that God never answered. Job's questions were simply a way for him to work through his grief. Then God asked Job questions—many questions. Job had no answers. After God's questions, Job saw God, himself, and his painful tribulation in a different light. Job accepted his place under the authority of the Almighty. He stopped climbing the ladder into the heavens trying to discern the purpose of God.

Help me, Lord, to remember, "Thy footsteps are not known" (Psalm 77:19). *I cannot anticipate your next move. I cannot understand your ways or change your purpose. My mind is human and finite.*

The more hopeless the situation, the more surprising are the ways of God. If I knew the end at the beginning, His way often would not seem so severe and treacherous. But if I knew the end at the beginning, I would never learn to stand still, trust, and rest in His direction of my affairs. If I knew the end at the beginning, God would not be God, and His mercy and grace would have little value. The difficult things in life, the unknown ways of God, challenge me and magnify God's mercy and grace. When God seems far away and the presence of His footsteps unperceived, He is nearer than I know. He is working in my heart.

Troubled times are learning and leaning and trusting times.
Trusting is leaning with all my weight on the Everlasting Arms.

QUESTIONS

1. Have I climbed up to look into God's council-chamber? What are the things I would like to know?
2. What are the best ways to draw near to God?

Listen

Be still, and know that I am God: I will be exalted among the heathen, I will be exalted in the earth. The LORD of hosts is with us; the God of Jacob is our refuge. Selah. Psalm 46:10–11

How hard it is to keep quiet and listen! When I am hurting, I find it easier to moan, groan, question, and blame. Yet I hear God saying I should be still and not try to work things out my way. It is easier to shove ahead without direction or to block the difficulty from my mind. However, God wants me to be still, with an open mind and a ready heart.

"There are occasions when man must stand aloof, and all must be left to the almighty Disposer of all things. It is for us to trust, commit, and be patient."[45]

If I would be still and listen, I might hear God telling me something that will encourage my heart.

- He may be trying to reassure and comfort me.
- He may have some words of direction for me.
- He may be calling me closer to His heart.
- He may be asking me to lay down my human reasoning.
- He may have some words of correction for me.

Help me, Lord, to be still so that . . .

- *I can KNOW that you are God.*
- *I can GROW into your image.*
- *I can SHOW others that you are God.*
- *I might GLOW in this dark world.*
- *I can BESTOW your love on hurting hearts.*

Sorrow defines the difference between happiness and joy.
Joy is inward, and not outward:
and so it does not depend on what we have,
but on what we are.

—Henry Van Dyke

QUESTIONS

1. Do I know how to be still and listen, or do I talk all the time?
2. Do I feel a need to keep people aware of my pain and my situation?
3. Am I searching for sympathy and understanding in the wrong places?
4. Why does God tell me to be still?
5. What have I learned by being still and listening?

Singing

Have mercy upon me, O LORD; for I am weak: O LORD, heal me; for my bones are vexed. My soul is also sore vexed: but thou, O LORD, how long? Return, O LORD, deliver my soul: oh save me for thy mercies' sake. For in death there is no remembrance of thee: in the grave who shall give thee thanks? I am weary with my groaning; all the night make I my bed to swim; I water my couch with my tears. Mine eye is consumed because of grief. Psalm 6:2-7

One day I scolded my canary, "You are not a very happy caged bird, are you? Where is your song?" Suddenly I realized the irony of my words. Neither was I a very happy caged bird! Grief and depression seemed to have me caged away from normal life, normal people, and normal thinking.

Indeed, I was very weak. My whole body was vexed—disturbed, troubled, and worn down. I was weary with my groaning. My eyes were painful because of tears. Would I ever learn to sing again?

My canary disturbed me because she would not sing. My daughter had brought her to me saying it would take a while for her to adjust to being alone, so she might not sing for a while. I thought she had had enough time to adjust, so she should be singing. I fed her, I gave her water, I cleaned her cage, and I even gave her treats. What else could she need? I thought she should be happy, for I was caring for her!

Again, I thought of my condition. Shouldn't I be singing God's praise? I thought of my Caregiver. Shouldn't I be happy? He has taken care of me in the past, He cares for me in the present, and He will care for me in the future.

When I complained about my canary's failure to sing, someone said, "Give her a little more time." I thought, *That is what I need, a little more time and a lot more positive thoughts!*

Dear Lord, help me! I am trying to learn to sing again—to sing alone! Singing lifts weights from the heart and removes fears from the mind. Singing relaxes my nerves and lowers my blood pressure. I must sing when the sky is dark and the pain is deep. I must sing of the God who loves and keeps me.

Brief is our life and filled with toil and care,
Though days be many or few
We connect with eternity through prayer.

—author unknown

Praise to God is honorable, especially when it comes through pain.

—author unknown

QUESTIONS

1. The psalmist felt a grief that affected his whole body. Certainly grief does affect the whole body, mind, and spirit. How have I been affected by my difficult experiences? I need to acknowledge the effects but not dwell on them.
2. What do music and singing do for me?
3. Do I put forth effort to sing praise to God?

Wait on God

I had fainted, unless I had believed to see the goodness of the LORD in the land of the living. Psalm 27:13

Because of his strength will I wait upon thee: for God is my defence. Unto thee, O my strength, will I sing: for God is my defence, and the God of my mercy. Psalm 59:9, 17

David said he would have fainted or despaired if he had not believed that he would see the goodness of the Lord in his present world, his present trial. By an effort of faith, David allowed the Lord to lift him from the depths of despair to the solid ground of the goodness of the Lord. What would have become of David if he had not believed? What will become of me if I do not believe in and search for the goodness of the Lord? Is it not the hope and help of God's love that prevents me from being crushed? Is it not His mercy and grace that see me through?

I must remind myself that God will not call me to fight an enemy I cannot conquer. He will not call me to bear a cross I cannot carry. He will not ask me to do something I have insufficient strength or knowledge to do. What I lack, He will supply.

God's formula for becoming strong is not self-confidence, self-assertion, or self-trust. Nor do I become strong by an easy life, independence, and liberty to follow my whims. God's formula for becoming strong is faith in the goodness of God. Only faith in a good God and a conscious choice to wait on Him will help me endure through trials.

When my heart is breaking with grief, "Wait upon God."
When my mind is clouded with confusion, "Wait upon God."
When tears of sorrow fill my eyes, "Wait upon God."
When a dozen emotions threaten to choke me, "Wait upon God."
When my will is in rebellion against the hard hand of God, "Wait upon God."

Why wait on God?

- Because only God has healing balm for my pain.
- Because only God has wisdom and perception to clear the confusion.
- Because only God truly understands and dries my tears with love.

- Because only God's mercy, grace, and strength will carry me through the deep, dark valley.
- Because only in submission and acceptance will I find peace.

When I wait upon the Lord, I will find that He is my strength.

When I wait on the Lord, I will learn that He is my defense.

When I wait on the Lord, I will have a song to sing of God's great mercies.

When I wait on the Lord, I still have faith and hope.

When I wait on the Lord, I can move forward in confidence and peace knowing that "He knoweth the way that I take: when he hath tried me, I shall come forth as gold" (Job 23:10).

God is good when life is pain.
God is good in sunshine or rain.
God is good when it seems He's not there.
God is good when it seems He's not fair.
God is good—because He is love!

QUESTIONS

1. What tools is God using to make me strong?
2. How do I hinder His work in making me strong?
3. What are some things I wish God would hurry up and do?
4. Why am I often in a hurry and God is never in a hurry?
5. What are some blessings I have received by waiting on God?

A Weaned Child

Surely I have behaved and quieted myself, as a child that is weaned of his mother: my soul is even as a weaned child. Psalm 131:2

When a child is deprived of his mother's milk, he experiences grief for the first time. It is a trial of patience. The child fusses and whines for what has been taken away. If weaning is such a painful time for the child and the mother, why wean the child? Because weaning is a part of the growing up process—a time to mature and get used to eating more substantial foods.

Job experienced excruciating pain during God's weaning process. He did not understand, did not enjoy, did not appreciate the process. Who would? Nevertheless, he kept his integrity. He clung to the reality of God's love and goodness, even when it didn't feel real to him. Later, when Job saw God in His greatness, he saw himself in his smallness. He said, "Therefore have I uttered that I understood not; things too wonderful for me, which I knew not. Wherefore I abhor myself, and repent in dust and ashes" (Job 42:3, 6). Job was a new man, a different man, a better man after God detached him from all earthly attachments.

Gerhard Tersteegen describes how God weans His children:

> The weaning of a child from its mother's breast, is not so useful to it, as when God our heavenly Father purposes to detach us, by means of the bitterness of this life, from the soul-destroying attachment to the things that are seen. Oh, it is infinite grace, when He breaks our wills and hedges up our way, not in order that we may be constrained to depart from him, but that we may run unto Him! Did we but recognize the high intentions of God towards us when He gives us pain, we would kiss the rod of His paternal love, and love Him and cleave to Him only the more cordially.[46]

When we lose our job, material security, home, or health, we experience loss—a weaning from something we value. Some face the loss not of what they had, but of what they never had. Some never had a marriage partner. Some never had a baby. Some never knew their birth parents. Some never had a strong, healthy body. What is our response when something we cherish is stripped away or something we long for is denied?

What am I doing with my loss? Am I handling it by God's grace and mercy, or is it managing my life and emotions? Am I willing to be weaned from my loss? How do I react in the face of strife, storm, death, and loss? I have found myself whining and fretful as a child who is being weaned. How much easier it is to lose when we voluntarily release what has been taken.

Lord, you have taken my husband and my daughters as part of your plan. I balk at these painful losses, these changes. Help me to submit even though I do not understand. Give me a heart of peaceful contentment and surrender to your will. Help me to stop whining and wanting my own way. Help me to recognize and appreciate your goodness and your wisdom. Help me to know that "all things work together for good to them that love God, to them who are the called according to his purpose" (Romans 8:28). *Truly, this weaning process has been for my betterment. Pain brings peace, grief produces growth, tears transport truth, fears turn into faith—all result in spiritual maturity when committed to you. Help me, Lord, to be content, even as a weaned child!*

QUESTIONS

1. From what is God weaning me?
2. How am I responding to the process of being weaned?
3. Do I truly feel God is good in the weaning that He allows?
4. What has been gained in this weaning process?

Responding Rightly

For thus saith the Lord GOD, the Holy One of Israel; In returning and rest shall ye be saved; in quietness and in confidence shall be your strength: and ye would not. Isaiah 30:15

Larry Crabb said, "In every situation, there's a way to respond that pleases God."[47]

O Lord, I think I am searching for the way to respond for your glory, but perhaps I am mostly searching for relief from my distress or answers to my questions.

The pain in my heart wonders, Why me, Lord? *How could you take two of my daughters and my husband, while my friends still have their children and husbands? Are you punishing me with this heartache? Am I worse than other women? Am I unworthy of loving relationships?*

These losses provoke some very unsettling questions, Lord. They also provoke a more trusting awareness of your work in my life. This confusion also has taken me off my throne of independence and laid me low at your feet. I cannot make it without you!

Lord, I do not understand why much of my life has been difficult, but I do know you are working. Truly, the fact that you are at work is more important than relief or answers. Being assured that you are working is in itself relief and an answer. I simply must remember and trust your work.

Larry Crabb also said, "Facing confusion honestly gives strong faith the opportunity to develop."[48] When life makes no sense, when confusion darkens our horizon, we can do one of three things.

1. We can forget our claim of Christianity and find instant and temporary relief in alcohol, drugs, or give up on life completely.
2. We can hide our questions, bury our emotions, and pretend we have found relief in the pat answers of some people's Christianity.
3. We can face our questions honestly, bring our confusion to a loving God, and cling to the claims of Christ's love, power, forgiveness, and comfort.

Lord, I choose to cling tenaciously to your love, power, forgiveness, and comfort.

> I am content. As thou didst test my faith, thou must supply the grace to keep me true.
> I walk in darkness—but I have thy word; I trust thy name;
> I know thee, Savior Lord, and lean upon my God to bring me through.
>
> —F.E.M. Irwin

When you don't understand,
When you can't see His plan,
When you can't trace His hand,
Trust His heart!

—Babbie Mason

QUESTIONS

1. Have I found the way to respond that pleases God?
2. What are my unsettling questions?
3. Which of the three ways described above have I chosen to help settle my confusion?
4. How do the opinions and judgments of others confuse or clarify my situation?

He Understands

[John] said unto [Jesus], Art thou he that should come,
or do we look for another? Matthew 11:3

Verily I say unto you, Among them that are born of women there hath not risen a greater than John the Baptist: notwithstanding he that is least in the kingdom of heaven is greater than he. Matthew 11:11

Lord, I thank you for understanding me when I question you. When John the Baptist sent his disciples with the question, "Or do we look for another?" you did not send a scathing message back to John. You did not say, "Surely, he knows I am the Christ! He saw the dove and heard the voice from heaven!" You did not say, "Tell John to snap out of it! A follower of God does not get depressed or ask such questions. What is he thinking? How can he be confused?"

Thank you, Jesus, for understanding John the Baptist's confusion. How good it was that he faced his confusion. How good it was that he had the courage to ask the question. You sent him a simple, kind answer to reassure his mind.

Thank you, Lord, for understanding me even when I do not understand myself. Let me never be offended because of what you allow to disrupt my life. Help me to trust when I am driven from my comfort zone into very uncomfortable situations.

Thank you for understanding my confusion and questions when I am dwelling in grief's prison, when I am sitting in the dungeon of despair, and when I am working through disappointments. Thank you for offering help, hope, and healing by loving, forgiving, and directing me in times of deep darkness. Thank you for always being there when I cry out for help!

A heart of compassion, with eyes of love,
Looks down from His throne in heaven above;
With tears of mercy and arms of grand grace,
He understands my pain with an embrace.
He wraps my confusion in His acclaim,
Receiving glory to His holy name.

—author unknown

Often we stand at life's crossroads
And view what we think is the end,

But God has a much bigger vision
And He tells us, "It's only a bend . . ."
—Helen Steiner Rice

QUESTIONS

1. Is it possible that John the Baptist was experiencing a time of depression? Why did he have questions about Jesus?
2. Based on the context of this passage, how does Jesus' reply to John the Baptist bring comfort to me?

Oil That Does Not Fail

And Elijah said unto her, Fear not; go and do as thou hast said: but make me thereof a little cake first, and bring it unto me, and after make for thee and for thy son. For thus saith the LORD God of Israel, The barrel of meal shall not waste, neither shall the cruse of oil fail, until the day that the LORD sendeth rain upon the earth. 1 Kings 17:13–14

Elijah asked the unthinkable of the poor widow. How many times I have thought God is asking the unthinkable of me! Why should I need to go through the valley of grief again while others have not been there once?

Elijah made an incredible promise to the widow. The widow, with daring faith, obeyed him. God, in His impossible way, kept His promise. The widow always had enough oil and meal during the famine.

How often has God poured in oil when my supply was gone?

- God's oil on my darkness generates light.
- God's oil on my weakness yields strength.
- God's oil on my despair brings hope.
- God's oil on my suffering results in comfort.
- God's oil on my pain provides relief.
- God's oil on my fearfulness gives courage.
- God's oil on my anger produces love.
- God's oil on my tears leads to joy.
- God's oil on death supplies life.

God's never-failing, ever-flowing oil is always available. I can either choose to accept and trust His work in my life, or choose to go my own way and depend on my own abilities to supply my needs.

What would have happened if the widow had not obeyed Elijah's request? She and her son would likely have died. She acted in obedience without knowing the result. That was faith!

When God asks for the first and the best, I will wither and die if I do not give it. He asks for the first and the best that He might give back to us the best that He has to offer.

In this world it is not what we take up,
but what we give up, that makes us rich.[49]
—Henry Ward Beecher

QUESTIONS

1. What are some of the unthinkable things that God has asked of me? How did I respond?
2. How should I respond to God when I don't understand His unthinkable requests?
3. Oil is used as a healer, a soother, and a softener. In what way do I need God's oil?

Shaken or Unshakable?

And this word, Yet once more, signifieth the removing of those things that are shaken, as of things that are made, that those things which cannot be shaken may remain. Hebrews 12:27

Things that can be shaken:

- Health
- Wealth
- Home
- Security
- Dreams
- Physical comforts
- Emotions
- Nations
- Beliefs
- Faith
- Denominations
- Mountains
- Trees
- Earth
- Sea

Things that cannot be shaken:

- God's kingdom "which cannot be moved" (Hebrews 12:28).
- God's Word—"[Jesus'] words shall not pass away" (Luke 21:33).
- "Jesus Christ the same yesterday, and to day, and for ever" (Hebrews 13:8).
- God's mercies are "new every morning" and cannot be moved (Lamentations 3:23).
- He who trusts in the Lord "shall not be moved" (Psalm 21:7).
- "[God] shall never suffer the righteous to be moved" (Psalm 55:22).

- God's grace cannot be shaken.
- God's truth cannot be shaken.

The shaking at Sinai was a sign of Jehovah's power and presence. When God shakes the heaven and the earth for the last time, no doubt will remain as to who is on the Rock and who is on the sand.

Lord, my life feels shaken to the very foundation. Oh, may I cling to the things that cannot be shaken! Help me, Lord, to be steadier through the storms of life. Give me strength to hang on.

I experienced a tremendous storm in my emotions today, Lord. I felt like my ship was sinking. I cried out to you for help, for hope, and for peace. A subtle change embraced my mind and enveloped my body. It was as if you said, "Peace, be still." Thank you, Lord, for the relief and release from the pressures and the crashes into despair. Thank you for bringing me into the harbor of your peace, time and time again. Keep me, Lord, anchored on the Rock.

The Lord does not keep me <u>from</u> life's storms
But He keeps me <u>in</u> life's storms.

QUESTIONS

1. What things have been shaken in my life?
2. What things have not been shaken?
3. What might my problem be if I become extremely shaken in the trials of life?
4. Is God in every storm? What part does God play in the storm? How does God deal with the storm? Based on Psalm 107:23–31, how should I feel about the storm?

My Times Are in Thy Hand

My times are in thy hand: deliver me from the hand of mine enemies, and from them that persecute me. Make thy face to shine upon thy servant: save me for thy mercies' sake. Psalm 31:15–16

Life is a journey taken but once. We do not get a chance to come back and try it over again in a different way. My times—the events of my birth, my death, the number of my days—are in your hand, dear Father. The seasons of joy, the seasons of sorrow, the days of hope, the nights of despair, the times of blessings, the times of adversity—all are in your hand.

My enemies, O Lord, are very different from David's enemies, but no less frightful and tortuous. My emotions persecute me night and day. My thoughts are in confusion. My body is in physical pain.

I need the smile of your face upon my dark path right now, Lord. Oh, teach me to be content and not to fret, to trust and not be afraid, to rest and not be anxious, to hope and not be impatient, to work and not be weary in well-doing.

When I rest assured that my times are in your hand, can I not be assured that the times of my loved ones are also in your hand? O Lord, help me to grasp the truth of this statement—my daughters' times were in your hand, my husband's times were in your hand. You have accomplished your plan for their lives, and you have called them home with you where time is no more.

He Knows

He knows it all—the winding path, the sky o'er cast and gray,
The steepness of the mountainside, the roughness of the way.

He knows it all—the haunting fear, the doubtings that distress,
The wond'rings and perplexities, and all the strain and stress.

He knows it all—each troubled thought, each anxious wave of care,
And every burden, every grief, or cross that thou dost bear.

He knows it all—thy weight of woe, thine often tear-dimmed eye,
The stabbing pain, the slow dull ache, and sorrow's broken cry.

He knows it all—but His to choose, and thine to take His choice!
He knows it all! He planned it so! Then trust Him, and rejoice!

—E. Margaret Clarkson

In your love I find submission.
In your goodness I find hope.
In your sovereignty I find trust.

QUESTIONS

1. What are some evidences that "my times are in His hands"?
2. What are some things about my life journey that I wish would never have happened? How did I deal with them? How should I deal with them so they do not hinder the remainder of my journey?

How Long?

And in the fourth watch of the night Jesus went unto them, walking on the sea. And when the disciples saw him walking on the sea, they were troubled, saying, It is a spirit; and they cried out for fear. But straightway Jesus spake unto them, saying, Be of good cheer; it is I; be not afraid. Matthew 14:25–27

Lord, how long? Lord, where are you? Lord, when will you help?

How often I chafe at the Lord's timing! How often I become impatient and demanding! Why does the Lord wait so long before He comes to my aid?

Why did He wait until the fourth hour to come to the aid of His struggling disciples? For almost nine hours they had been fighting for their lives against the wild sea. Perhaps their minds were so filled with their struggle in the fierce storm that they did not even wonder where Jesus was. They were good sailors; they had fought many a storm. They could win this battle. Or could they? Their strength was failing! They were exhausted! They were fearful! They were about ready to give up.

Then they saw it! Was it a spirit? It spoke, "Be of good cheer; it is I; be not afraid" (Matthew 14:27).

I doubt that the disciples questioned Jesus. I think they simply relaxed and enjoyed His presence and peace. Perhaps they realized why Jesus had not come sooner. Maybe they understood that they had been trusting in their own strength, their own experiences of success, their own management abilities. Perhaps they had not learned the power of prayer and the necessity of calling out to God for help. All they knew was, they had come to the end of themselves, the end of their ability and strength. That was when Jesus came!

That is always when Jesus comes. When I get to the end of myself, the end of my resources, the end of my independence—then is when Jesus comes, giving me aid, comfort, and direction.

QUESTIONS

1. Does Jesus always come and calm my storm as soon as I think He should?

2. Are there any things I should do or attitudes I should foster while I wait for Jesus to calm my storm?
3. When do I become impatient with God's timing?
4. What do I do when I become impatient?

PART THREE

LOOKING AHEAD

Look Ahead

It's hard to face the future
When God calls a loved one home;
Back into the past you let
Your happy memories roam.
But do not feed yourself too long
On sorrow's bitter bread;
Life goes on, and it demands
That you must look ahead.
It's sad to walk the road alone
Instead of side by side.
When the ways divide,
Try then to remember
That the dear one who has gone
Would have you turn
Toward the sunshine,
Passing bravely on.

—author unknown

My Shepherd

The LORD is my shepherd. Psalm 23:1

From childhood, most of us have learned Psalm 23 by memory, but many of us never experience it profoundly until later in life. Life events teach us different aspects of the Lord as our Shepherd, but we truly experience the Lord as our Shepherd when we pass through the valley of the shadow of death. It seems that only in difficult trials do we learn to fully depend on Him. Only when we have no strength of our own do we rely on His. Shame on us! How must the almighty God feel when He is just waiting for us to ask Him for help?

When David said, "The Lord is my shepherd," what did he mean?

THE Lord is my Shepherd. THE—not a lord, or some lord, or this lord, or that lord, nor whatever lord. He is THE Lord—special, specific, the one and only Lord.

The LORD is my Shepherd. The LORD Jehovah, the self-existing One, the supreme God, the exalted One, the Creator of all mankind, the Creator of this mighty universe and all that is in it. He is my Owner, my Master, my Savior, my Shepherd.

The Lord IS my Shepherd. He IS. This is a fact, a positive statement. He IS right now—not was, will be, may be, might be, should be—He IS my shepherd!

The Lord is MY shepherd. He is MY personal shepherd. Mine. I belong to Him and He belongs to me. He is special to me and I am special to Him.

The Lord is my SHEPHERD. He is my Good Shepherd, my One and only Shepherd, my Great Shepherd, my Chief Shepherd, my seeking Shepherd, my caring and carrying Shepherd, and my loving Shepherd. He is my particular, claimed, individual, sustaining, protecting, and empathizing Shepherd. The Lord is my SHEPHERD.

> I am a sheep who needs tender care,
> For I have a load I cannot bear.
> I need the Shepherd to feel with me
> The depths of my loss and agony.
> Jesus, my Shepherd, brings love and hope;
> In His steadfast light I do not grope.
> He is the way, the truth, and the life;
> He is my defender in daily strife.

QUESTIONS

1. In what ways has the Lord proven Himself my Shepherd?
2. Am I a good sheep? What qualities and behaviors are characteristic of a good sheep?
3. When I am going through a dark valley, it is sometimes difficult to feel that the Shepherd is with me. Sometimes I may need to do things to encourage myself. What are some supportive acts I can do for myself on dark days?
4. "And he said unto me, My grace is sufficient for thee: for my strength is made perfect in weakness. Most gladly therefore will I rather glory in my infirmities, that the power of Christ may rest upon me. Therefore I take pleasure in infirmities, in reproaches, in necessities, in persecutions, in distresses for Christ's sake: for when I am weak, then am I strong" (2 Corinthians 12:9–10). What do these verses mean to me?

I Shall Not Want

I shall not want. Psalm 23:1

"I shall not want!" This is a mouthful when my heart is breaking and I am experiencing a tremendous loss—be it a death, a broken relationship, a financial or natural disaster, or a physical or mental illness. To say or even think "I shall not want" seems impossible when my entire being struggles to survive the present pain. A multitude of needs asserts itself in my mind. A host of desires surges through my thoughts.

I will stop, turn my attention to God, and try to comprehend what "I shall not want" means in my time of severest trial. When Jesus is my Good Shepherd, it means I will not lack provision, fulfillment, or companionship. I will be satisfied with His direction—the path on which He leads me. I will pray for submission to what I do not understand.

Jesus, in the Garden of Gethsemane, felt heart-wrenching anguish so intense that He sweat great drops of blood. He placed His agony into His Father's hands and cried out, "Not as I will, but as thou wilt" (Matthew 26:39). The weight of the sins of the world—past, present, and future—lay on His shoulders. Still, in His bitterest hour of pain, He found peace and relief in surrender to His Father's will.

As humans, we have many needs, but our Good Shepherd's resources are limitless! Our finite minds cannot fathom the infinite riches of our Shepherd. Yet we have an intellectual knowledge of God's ability to do the best for us. For me, the problem sometimes lies in my ego: *I can take care of myself. I can think for myself. I can make my own decisions.* Then something huge and uncontrollable, something horribly painful comes into my life. Where do I turn for help? Where do I look for relief? When I fall in brokenness before my Good Shepherd, He assures me that I will not lack anything.

Thank you, Lord, for reminding me to come to you with my needs. Help those who do not know where to go with their deep needs. When they turn to drugs, alcohol, sex, or other forms of self-gratification, turn their emptiness into a longing to know you. O Lord, help me to share with other longing souls my satisfaction with you. In my greatest hour of need, may I find fulfillment in surrender to your will.

QUESTIONS

1. What are my greatest needs or wants today?
2. How did Jesus deal with the great need He felt in the garden of Gethsemane? Did He also express a want?
3. What areas of my life do I need to surrender?
4. If I am not surrendered to God in only one area of my life, will I be hopeful about the future or satisfied with His will?

Free in His Care

He maketh me to lie down in green pastures. Psalm 23:2

He makes me lie down and rest in the awareness of His presence and care. He draws me away from the wild rush and roar of living and makes me relax in His protection.

My Shepherd has many ways of drawing me aside. He may use sickness, financial disaster, broken relationships, or grief to stop my whirling world and cause me to realize there is more to life than what I have been experiencing. He whispers in my ear, ***"Come unto me and rest"*** (Matthew 11:28). ***"Be still, and know that I am God"*** (Psalm 46:10). His presence and His still, small voice dispel my fear and panic.

In the middle of the wasteland of trials and tribulations, He has prepared green pastures for me. They are pastures where He has removed the stumps of self-conceit, roots of bitterness, and weeds of unbelief, envy, discouragement, and dissatisfaction. He has sown there His seeds of love, mercy, forgiveness, hope, and grace. His pastures are exceedingly rich, lavishly green, and truly productive.

In His care, I am free:

- Free from fear—not alarmed by hidden enemies or dangers.
- Free from panic and the terror of being unable to cope—finding the Shepherd to be my refuge, my hiding place, my strong tower, my keeper, my guide.
- Free from agitation—unperturbed by pests (slander, accusations, or guilt) that cause tension and unrest. His presence is my quietness and strength.
- Free from rivalry—unfretted by jealousy, competition, or peer pressure. When I have died to myself, He is the source of my life. He alone is my contentment.
- Free from hunger—nourished on the green pastures of His Word that are completely satisfying when I obey His commands and trust His promises.
- Free from desperation—encouraged to face whatever tomorrow brings, knowing that He loves me, lives for me, and cares for me.

When I choose to rest in His green pastures, my strength is renewed, my heavenly focus is sharpened, and my mind is stayed on Him.

Yes, there are green pastures even in the valley of the shadow of death. In deep grief, it is possible to find great comfort in the care of the Good Shepherd. When I simply acknowledge my need for sustenance and rest in His green pastures, He meets my needs.

> Man needs both solitude and prayer.
> By all means, use some time to be alone.
> Salute thyself; see what thy soul doth wear.
>
> —George Herbert

QUESTIONS

1. From what pests (emotions or burdens) do I need freedom?
2. What are the green pastures to me? Have I learned to lie down in the Shepherd's green pastures?
3. How do I feel about my Shepherd's care during my valley experience? What do I see and feel as His care or lack of care? Since I believe there is no lack with Him, why do I deal with negative feelings at times?

Still Waters

He leadeth me beside the
still waters. Psalm 23:2

Can I find still waters in the midst of turbulent emotions? Can I drink from still waters in the depths of this heartache and pain? The Shepherd always makes still waters available. Where do I go to try to quench my thirst? I may choose to anesthetize my troubled mind by reading unhealthy books with humanistic teaching and unrealistic thinking, or I may refresh my mind with the truth of God's character and Word or by reading challenging true stories of others' trials and victories.

Why does a shepherd lead the sheep beside still waters? Sheep will not drink from rough, stormy waters. But they will drink from mucky, disease-filled, contaminated puddles. To keep them healthy and to quench their thirst, the shepherd leads them to still, clear waters.

Similarly, the Lord, my Shepherd, knows my need for refreshment. "Blessed are they which do hunger and thirst after righteousness: for they shall be filled" (Matthew 5:6). He makes it His business to satisfy me.

My Shepherd offers me pure, quiet, fresh, thirst-quenching waters; beside them I can relax, meditate, and commune with Him. He leads me away from the strain and stress of my labor. He draws me aside from my confused thoughts and painful ponderings. "He leadeth me beside the still waters." When I come to the end of my resources, when I feel devoid of strength or the ability to go on—He leads me to His tranquil, cool waters.

He leads me beside the still waters that quench my thirst. They . . .

- Calm and quiet my anxiety.
- Align my thoughts with His thoughts.
- Supply my innermost needs.
- Refresh and rebuild my strength.
- Reconstruct my jumbled feelings into peaceful patterns.

QUESTIONS

1. Where do I go to quench my thirst?
2. What do I do to anesthetize my troubled mind?
3. In what ways does God's Word quench my thirst and give me satisfaction?
4. What is the deepest longing of my heart right now? How do I expect it to be satisfied?

Cast Down

He restoreth my soul. Psalm 23:3

Why art thou cast down, O my soul? and why art thou disquieted in me? hope thou in God: for I shall yet praise him for the help of his countenance. Psalm 42:5

David knew what it was to be "cast down" himself, and as a shepherd, he knew what a "cast" sheep was. Likely most humans have known that cast-down feeling at some time. A cast sheep and a cast human are both helpless, vulnerable to attack by predators, and close to death.

When David says, "He restoreth my soul," he is speaking of the shepherd stooping and lifting the cast sheep to his feet again. Sheep can become cast when they lie down in a comfortable hollow, have too much wool, or become too fat.

Who needs restoration? A cast sheep needs restoration, and so does the cast Christian: the fatigued father, the melancholy mother, the cranky child, the unyielding youth, the bustling businessman, the troubled teacher, the unproductive preacher, and the hurting mourner. Even though we are in our loving Shepherd's wonderful care, we still need restoration at times. Our earthly minds, bodies, and souls often need to be restored, no matter what the cause of our distress.

- When I am cast down with discouragement and dejection, He pulls me from the miry clay of self-pity and places me at His feet again.
- When I find that soft, comfortable spot, that easy place, and I fall for lack of self-discipline, He may remove some of my comfort in order to restore my soul again.
- When I become bogged down with the self-life (that thick-cushioned wool) and with worldly things that cling to me so I cannot move forward, He cuts away the wool and restores my soul.
- When my business, career, or family have flourished and I become "fat" with self-assurance and fall flat, He puts me on an humble diet and restores my soul.
- When I fail my spouse, my children, my brothers and sisters, or my Lord, He feeds me on His forgiveness and restores my soul.
- When duties, cares, trials, lack of fulfillment, or defeat cast me into despair, He lifts me with His love and mercy, and gives me a reason for living. He restores my soul.

- When I walk through the dark valley of grief, pain, or turmoil, my entire being needs daily restoration. Awareness of His presence and His faithfulness help heal my broken heart and restore my soul.

Thank you, dear Shepherd, for having an eye for cast sheep!

QUESTIONS

1. Why am I cast down?
2. What enemies stalk me when I am cast?
3. How will I get back on my feet again?
4. What areas of my life need restoration?
5. There are no self-helps, no magic pills, and no renewal programs that will restore my soul. Am I convinced that only God is able to restore? What is the part I play in that restoration? (Refer to page 296, Appendix B.)

Right Paths

He leadeth me in the paths of righteousness
for his name's sake. Psalm 23:3

When trials cast me down, the Shepherd sets me back on my feet, placing my feet on right paths. I may choose to wander from the right paths, or I may choose to follow in His footsteps.

"Paths of righteousness for his name's sake" means . . .

- Things in my life may be unfair, but He does all things in righteousness.
- Righteous living for His glory is possible.
- God makes no mistakes!

God will always do what is right for me because He is a just God. He is jealous of His name, His character, and His glory. "For thou shalt worship no other god: for the LORD, whose name is Jealous, is a jealous God" (Exodus 34:14).

God leads me. He does not drive me. He does not chase me. He does not push me or pull me. He leads me, and when the way gets rough, He carries me.

Like a sheep, I have poor eyesight and little sense of direction. I need my Shepherd to lead me.

He always leads me in right paths—not rose-petal-covered paths, or plush, carpeted paths. Sometimes it is a steep path, sometimes a rocky trail. Sometimes it is a sunny road, other times a thorn-covered way or a dark passage. He knows the path I need for each season of my life. He leads me onward victoriously, magnifying His name in the process.

"He leadeth me in the paths of righteousness for his name's sake." He gets glory to His name by His dealings with His sheep. He gets glory to His name when I choose to live a righteous, pure life. Yes, for His name's sake, the darker the passage may mean more glory to His name. The more treacherous the path may mean more honor to His way. The holier my life, the more honor to His name. I can choose to trust and follow the careful leading of my Good Shepherd.

No pain, no gain, no glory to His name!

QUESTIONS

1. Am I walking in righteousness right now?
2. How much control does God have over my life?
3. Are there areas in my life that I do not allow God to control? What are they?
4. Does my life reflect glory to or shame on the name of God?

Through the Valley

Yea, though I walk through the valley of the shadow of death, I will fear no evil. Psalm 23:4

I walk *through* the valley. The valley is not a place to move into and stay! The valley is not a place to become satisfied and accustomed to for a lifetime. The Lord does not intend for the valley to be a dead end.

Lord, I will remember . . .

- *You know the way before me.*
- *You promised to go with me: "Lo, I am with you alway"* (Matthew 28:20).
- *You are leading me to higher ground. The most nourishing grass grows on higher ground, and we have to pass through the valley to get to higher ground. Every life has many valleys, though some are deeper and darker than others. Some people have many more valleys than others have. I will not doubt your plan for getting me to higher ground.*
- *You are in complete control of all things.*
- *Even death is but a shadow and a valley leading to the bright golden morning of eternal life.*

I will not fear the dark valley. I will not try to detour around it, for it is in the dark valley that your mercy, love, and guidance radiate most brightly. In the dark valley my faith is renewed, and my hope is strengthened. In the valley, I grow.

I will fear no evil because you are with me in every situation. You are my Protector, Guide, and Shepherd. Your presence is full of power. Because you have overcome the world, I shall overcome the world. I shall overcome the grief of this valley. You are a God of goodness, love, truth, righteousness, peace, light, and salvation. I will fear no evil.

God without man is still God;
Man without God is nothing.
—author unknown

QUESTIONS

1. What does God want me to do with my valleys?
2. In what ways does my valley distress me?
3. What facts about God give me the confidence to trust Him?
4. What am I learning in my valley?

Survivor or Conqueror?

In all these things we are more than conquerors through him that loved us. Romans 8:37

In 1912 when the "unsinkable" Titanic sank, there were approximately 705 survivors. The sea became the grave for about 1,500.

I seriously doubt that the survivors felt like honored, successful, victorious people. In fact, some of the men who survived were shunned and classed as cowards because they jumped into lifeboats that should have been reserved for the women and children.

Being a survivor can carry bad memories and deep scars which haunt a person for life. The word *survive* or *survivor* is not in the Bible, but the words *conquer* and *conquerors* are. When we face trauma and pain, we must choose whether to adopt the mentality of a survivor or of a conqueror.

A conqueror is a victor, one who obtains booty from the strife. He comes away with treasures and honor. A conqueror may leave the battle with scars, but these only add to the honor of his victory.

As Christ goes forth to conquer, He goes with Calvary's scars, but He is ever victorious in conquering sin and Satan. Moreover, He challenges us to be more than conquerors.

Can I leave the dark valley of loss, the painful valley of sickness, the fearful valley of terror, carrying with me lessons I learned about the character of the Good Shepherd who walked these valleys with me? Can I walk away from a severe trial as a conqueror, with a smile on my face and a song in my heart? Do my tears purge away bitterness and anger? Can I give the shattered pieces of my heart to the Great Physician for His restoring touch and keep returning to Him for forgiveness and healing?

Great conquerors in the kingdom of God are not always the strongest, bravest, most honorable; usually they are the meekest, weakest, most fully dependent on the Master.

Help me, Lord, to remember that you will make me a great conqueror as long as I cling in faith to your strength. Oh, make me a conqueror, not just a survivor!

Courage wins! It always wins! Though days be slow,
And nights be dark 'twixt days that come and go,
Still courage will win; its average is sure;
He gains the prize who will the most endure;
Who faces issues; he who never shirks;
Who waits and watches, and who always works.

—author unknown

Courage

Courage isn't having strength to go on . . .
It is going on when you don't have strength.
Courage isn't going just where the light is . . .
It's following through the dark valleys.
Courage isn't being so big that you're not afraid . . .
It's moving ahead when you are afraid.
Courage isn't accepting yourself when you feel good . . .
It's accepting yourself when your friends misunderstand you.
Courage is standing with God amidst trials and opposition
Without feeling very courageous.

—author unknown

QUESTIONS

1. Am I living as a survivor or a conqueror?
2. If I am a conqueror, what is my booty from the strife (my gains from the trial)?
3. What gives me courage?
4. Is my idea of courage correct?

Shadows and Light

Who is among you that feareth the LORD, that obeyeth the voice of his servant, that walketh in darkness, and hath no light? let him trust in the name of the LORD, and stay upon his God. Isaiah 50:10

Mary Gardiner Brainard once said, "I would rather walk in the dark with God than go alone in the light."

I always thought of the valley as a place of darkness, but that is not necessarily the case. Some days seem dark, but there is always some light. Doesn't every valley receive some sunlight? Clouds may pass over, causing shadows, and surrounding mountains cast shadows, but light must be present in order to create shadows.

My thinking patterns can create dark clouds or sunshine. Some days clouds of doubt, anxiety, self-will, self-confidence, or lack of confidence come between me and my source of Son-light.

In the valley I am often reminded, "It is not in man that walketh to direct his steps" (Jeremiah 10:23). I cannot see but one step at a time because that is all I can handle. Thank you, Lord, for understanding my humanity! To know the future could be devastating, distracting, or debilitating. Yet my human nature longs to take a peek into what is ahead. However, my merciful, all-wise Shepherd leads me on one step at a time with just enough light to keep me from stumbling.

Help me, Lord, has been my daily prayer many times throughout the day while traveling this valley. John Ashworth says of this prayer, "It will fit in everywhere and to everything. It sums up all our need. It appropriately meets us whatever may be our circumstances."[50]

"For the Lord GOD will help me; therefore shall I not be confounded: therefore have I set my face like a flint, and I know that I shall not be ashamed" (Isaiah 50:7). To "set my face like a flint" means that I am determined, looking neither to the left or right, but fixed on the promises of God. May my confidence ever be in God and my face always be set like a flint!

All that I am, e'en here on earth,
All that I hope to be
When Jesus comes, and glory dawns,
I owe it, Lord, to thee.[51]

—Horatius Bonar

QUESTIONS

1. What circumstances, people, or attitudes are creating clouds in my life?
2. Have I ever tried to move ahead of God? What happened when I did?
3. Have I "set my face like a flint" according to the above definition?
4. What has given me light in this valley?

Be Not Afraid

For they all saw him, and were troubled. And immediately he talked with them, and saith unto them, Be of good cheer: it is I; be not afraid. Mark 6:50

"Be not afraid" and "fear not" are common phrases throughout the Bible. In fact, they are so common that they add up to one "fear not" or "be not afraid" for each day of the year. God knew that our lives on earth could be filled with fears, but He desires that we be not afraid.

The disciples of Jesus found it easy not to fear while walking with their Master beside the sea, sitting with the multitudes listening to Him teach, or passing out the miracle meal to the five thousand. But when Jesus compelled them to get into the ship and leave Him, they found themselves alone, rowing hard in contrary winds. In the midst of the storm, they saw what looked like a spirit walking on the water. Suddenly they were very much afraid.

Jesus' words, "Be of good cheer: it is I; be not afraid," turned their fear into amazed wonder and peace.

Dear Lord, when I fear
the dark valley,
the lonely nights,
the bridge between here and the future,
the sudden surges of grief,
the feeling of not being needed,
the feeling of not being cared for,
my inability to cope,
having no one to share with,
the sad aloneness—

May I find your "Fear not, be not afraid," as a light brightening my pathway, lifting my heart, calming my doubts, and erasing my fears.

Under the shadow of your wings let me hide,
Till you have stilled the storm and calmed the tide!

QUESTIONS

1. What fears am I dealing with during this trial?
2. How does fear cause bondage?
3. Fear often stirs up other emotions. What emotions do I need to manage because of my fears?
4. How should my knowledge of God help me with my fears? (Refer to "The Attributes of God," page 291, Appendix A.)

Griefs of God's Sending

Fear none of those things which thou shalt suffer: behold, the devil shall cast some of you into prison, that ye may be tried; and ye shall have tribulation ten days: be thou faithful unto death, and I will give thee a crown of life. Revelation 2:10

Life's trials, sorrows, complexities, struggles, and persecution will not last forever. A little while, and it will be over! Paul Gerhardt wrote, "Griefs of God's sending all have an ending . . . Sunshine will come when the tempest is past."[52]

Gerhardt wisely points out that only God-sent griefs, trials, and afflictions have an ending. Only God can guarantee betterment after pain, recovery after trials, and growth after afflictions. Only God can bring sunshine after storm, peace after turmoil, and light after darkness.

When we create our own griefs and struggles, they go on with us through life unless we seek God's forgiveness and surrender to His will. How many griefs are the result of human failure, yet God is blamed! How much of my pain have I caused? How many of my trials have I created by my stubbornness or selfishness? How often is my way dark because I refuse to follow the light?

I must remember—I am in a valley, not in a box. There is a way through the valley. Grief, pain, and affliction are not to be evaded or endured, but embraced. I must stop asking, "Why am I in this valley?" and begin asking, "What can I learn in this valley?"

"Griefs of God's sending" are His tools of refinement. Some of our most valuable lessons are learned in His school of affliction. During the difficult times we can develop a loving, trusting relationship with our Creator. When we are right with God, we have nothing to fear. Trials and pain become the golden pathway to glory. The crown of life is promised to those who faithfully endure.

Lord, I want to do better than just endure. Help me to submit to, accept, and conquer whatever you send into my life. Help me to remember that death dies in the grave and eternal life begins. A crown of life is waiting for those who overcome. Make me an overcomer, Lord!

Sorrows and trials build the shining, excruciating ladder on which my soul climbs nearer to God.

QUESTIONS

1. What are some griefs of my own making that I have endured?
2. What is the difference between God-sent griefs and griefs I have caused?
3. What factors contribute to making my own grief?
4. How do I find relief from grief I have caused myself?

Yielded to God in Meekness

The LORD will give strength unto his people; the LORD will bless his people with peace. Psalm 29:11

I must realize my weakness before God will make me strong. I must be of one mind with God before I can have peace. In grief, at times it is difficult to be of one mind with God. My fleshly mind wants to figure out all the ways things could have been different, all the ways life would be easier if things had been different, all the reasons why things ought not be as they are. Yes, the fleshly mind is at enmity with God and with the spiritual mind. Only a spiritual mind established in faith and flooded with the facts of God's wonderful character can be of one mind with God.

Strength and peace are what I need to make it through each day. When I choose to function in God's strength throughout the day, I will rest with a peaceful heart each night.

Place
Every
Anxiety in
Christ's
Efficiency

"But the meek shall inherit the earth; and shall delight themselves in the abundance of peace" (Psalm 37:11).

Another aspect of strength and peace is meekness. Meekness has been called "gentle strength" and "controlled strength." Meekness is my need of the hour when my mind goes into a tailspin trying to figure out the whys of God's ways.

Help me, Lord, to realize I do not have to know why I am in this dark valley, this difficult place, out of my comfort zone. Help me to accept that I do not have to understand your ways and reasons. The spirit of meekness will be my strength, bringing my soul into peace with you.

- I need a meek tongue—one that does not charge God foolishly.
- I need a meek mind—one that accepts God's thoughts and ways as sovereign.

- I need a meek heart—one that recognizes that God's purpose is for my good.

My job in life is to take care of the possibles
and to trust God with the impossibles.

QUESTIONS

1. In what situations do I need the strength of God to see me through?
2. What brings me peace of heart and mind?
3. In what areas am I finding it difficult to be of one mind with God?
4. How does a meek spirit bring me into harmony with God?
5. How can I place every anxiety in Christ's efficiency? Is this easy for me to do?

Better Than the Birds

Behold the fowls of the air: for they sow not, neither do they reap, nor gather into barns; yet your heavenly Father feedeth them. Are ye not much better than they? Matthew 6:26

Jesus asks a number of questions in Matthew 6:25–34. Is not your life more important than food and the body more than clothing? Why do you worry about what you will wear? Why do you worry about what you will eat? Are you not better than the birds? What can you add to your life by anxious thoughts? In short, Jesus is asking, "Since I take care of the birds, the flowers, and the grass, why do you worry over temporal things?"

Do I find it difficult to believe that I am more important than the birds, flowers, and the grass? Surely not! Since God cares about the comfort and welfare of the little creatures, is He not good enough and great enough to take care of me? Too often I respond as though God's mercies are not a reality in my life. God is good! This is a wonderful thought that I need to remember. God is good, and what He does is good.

Bad things, sickness, and death happen because of sin. God allows natural disasters, disease, and death; but in the lives of His children He uses these tragedies for our good.

Perhaps the birds can sing because they are ignorant of the future. As humans, we have the ability to think ahead. Sometimes thinking about the future makes us despondent and fearful. Why did God give us the think-ahead ability? Certainly not to make us miserable! When I consider the future with the fear of the Lord in my heart, I will not be miserable or fearful. I can acknowledge His greatness and goodness. This infuses hope and trust into my situation, no matter how difficult it may seem.

O thou bounteous Giver of all good,
Thou art of all thy gifts thyself the crown!
Give what thou canst, without thee we are poor;
And with thee rich, take what thou wilt away.

—William Forsyth

QUESTIONS

1. What thoughts of tomorrow are worrying me now?
2. What is the cause of worry?
3. How does my life demonstrate the fear of the Lord or the lack of it?

A Fresh Start

If any man be in Christ, he is a new creature: old things are passed away; behold, all things are become new. 2 Corinthians 5:17

I wish there were some wonderful place
Called the land of beginning again,
Where all our mistakes and all our heartaches,
And all our selfish grief
Could be dropped like a shabby coat at the door
And never put on again.
—Lolita Hiroshi

There is a land of beginning again, of new starts, of change and growth. The gateway to beginning again lies at the throne of God's mercy. There, in forgiveness and love, He removes our sins and casts them into the depths of the sea. He heals our heartaches as we trust Him. He gives us strength to go on, assured that our faith in Christ's atonement is imputed to us for righteousness.

God not only gives humanity a chance to begin again, but He also gives the rest of His creation the chance to begin again. In the fall, trees shed leaves and grow fresh spring green ones the next year. The birds and other animals lose feathers and hairy coats that are replaced with fine new costumes. The fuzzy caterpillar experiences what is perhaps the most dramatic transformation in the natural world when he emerges from his cocoon as a beautiful butterfly.

Only God can renew nature. Only God can perform that change in the caterpillar. Only God can bring about transformation in us. Only God can close the door on the old and open the pathway to the new. Only God can hand me a fresh, unspoiled day and say, "Do better, my child."

Do Better Now, My Child

He came to my desk with a quivering lip,
The lesson was done.
"Have you a new sheet for me, dear teacher?
I've spoiled this one."
I took his sheet, all soiled and blotted,
And gave him a new one all unspotted,
And to his tired heart I cried,
"Do better now, my child."

I went to the throne with a troubled heart,
The day was done.
"Have you a new day for me, dear Master?
I've spoiled this one."
He took my day, all soiled and blotted,
And gave a new one all unspotted.
And to my tired heart He cried,
"Do better now, my child."

—Kathleen Wheeler

QUESTIONS

1. In what ways does God provide renewal for my body?
2. In what areas of my life do I need to begin again?
3. God can give me a clean sheet to start each day only when I do my part. What is my part?
4. Why am I thankful for the chance to begin again?

Questions or Exclamations?

These all died in faith, not having received the promises, but having seen them afar off, and were persuaded of them, and embraced them, and confessed that they were strangers and pilgrims on the earth. For they that say such things declare plainly that they seek a country. Hebrews 11:13–14

Suppose the elderly continued to grow older, their aches and pains only getting worse—but could not die. Suppose the sick person continued to grow sicker and sicker—but could not die. Suppose the man with dementia would get more erratic by the month—but could not die. Living on and on in pain and disease would be a thousand times worse than dying, at least for the Christian. Not only would such situations be torture for the old and the sick, but also for the loved ones who cared for them.

If we can look at death from this angle, we can see in death the wise purpose of God. In this sinful world, deathlessness would be a scourge beyond our ability to handle. For the Christian, death is a gift from God to end earth's pain and to begin eternity's peace and joy.

What is the secret of dying gracefully? Is it not to live my life so there are no questions at my funeral or graveside—no questions about my life's purpose, no questions as to my destiny? I want to live my life with exclamation marks and periods.

This person was a child of God!
This person said no to Satan and sin!
This person spent her life serving others.
This person told others about her Savior.
This person went about doing good.

What will be said about me after I am gone? What kind of memorial am I building? What kind of legacy am I leaving? What kinds of memories, what kinds of statements, what kinds of questions am I making in the minds and hearts of those whom I love and who love me? My life will continue to speak after my lips have been silenced by death, just as Abel of whom it is said, "He being dead yet speaketh" (Hebrews 11:4).

Need thee the praise of love-written sonnet;
The name and the epitaph graved on the stone?
The things we have lived for, let them be our story,
And we but remembered by what we have done.

—author unknown

Death is the foreshadowing of life.
We die that we may die no more.

QUESTIONS

1. What if my life would change no more? Would I be happy if everything remained as it is now?
2. What changes, if any, do I need to make in my choices to help assure my family and friends of the direction of my life?
3. At my funeral, what do I think I might be remembered for?
4. In what ways do I believe death is a gift from God?

Love Gives Power

Jesus said unto him, Thou shalt love the Lord thy God with all thy heart, and with all thy soul, and with all thy mind. This is the first and great commandment. And the second is like unto it, Thou shalt love thy neighbour as thyself. Matthew 22:37-39

Jesus was asked, "Master, which is the great commandment in the law?" (Matthew 22:36). Jesus showed His greatness as a teacher by summing up the whole duty of man in a few words, "Thou shalt love the Lord thy God with all thy heart, and with all thy soul, and with all thy mind." This is unadulterated devotion. These simple words leave no room for misunderstanding or offense. Too often the religious leaders of Jesus' time chose their own ideas and rules instead of God's. Jesus leaves no room for competition. To love Him with every part of my being means full surrender—no room for my own ideas or rules.

When a man loves God with his whole being, he will love his neighbor as himself. On these two commandments hangs all religious and moral law.

What is the essence of love? Jesus could not have used a more comprehensive word. Think for a moment of the implications if Jesus had said, "Thou shalt fear the Lord thy God," or "Thou shalt hope in the Lord thy God," or "Thou shalt trust the Lord thy God." Fear, hope, and trust are necessary for a proper relationship with God, yet none of them are as all-encompassing as love.

Love is tender, unselfish, divine devotion. The emotion and warmth of love is directed toward another person. Love seeks to please its object with all its power. From love spring spontaneous service and obedience.

God so loved us that He gave His only Son to die for us. Jesus' suffering on the cross is the essence of love. In view of God's supreme sacrifice for us, it is imperative that we love Him supremely, without reservation. Since God is sovereign, He has the authority to demand that we love Him with all our power—heart, mind, soul, and strength.

Moreover, when we love God with our whole being, love's all-inclusive power will overflow to those around us. If we have a lack of love toward our neighbor, it is time to look at our love for God. The measure of our love for God is never greater than our love for the person we love the least.

The power of Christ's love in my life will make me speak in gentler tones. His love will help me think more kindly of others. His love will prompt me to respond more quickly and wholeheartedly to the needs around me. Love will keep me from wrapping myself up in a shroud of sorrow and ignoring the needs of others. Love will keep me tender in my touch and tone.

QUESTIONS

1. Why is love the greatest commandment?
2. How can love help me deal with my pain?
3. What areas of my life are lacking in love?
4. How can I show love to my family? Friends? Other hurting people? God?
5. What does 1 Corinthians 13 tell me about love?

A Fruitful Tree

Blessed is the man that trusteth in the LORD, and whose hope the LORD is. For he shall be as a tree planted by the waters, and that spreadeth out her roots by the river, and shall not see when heat cometh, but her leaf shall be green; and shall not be careful in the year of drought, neither shall cease from yielding fruit. Jeremiah 17:7-8

These verses depict the child of God as God desires him to be. It is the picture of what I long to be. How do I achieve that desire?

The secret is in my anchor. The two anchors for the life rooted and grounded in God are trust and hope in God. These anchors are welded inseparably into one. Without these anchor roots, I will fail and fall. I will not become a strong, beautiful tree. What will trust and hope do for me?

- Grow me—As roots grow deeper, branches spread broader. Spirit life and plant life can never be inactive for long. When growth ceases, decay takes over. Even the pain and sorrow of my heart will produce growth if I allow it. *Keep me growing, Lord!*
- Beautify me—Growth creates beauty. Living, fresh shades of green revive and calm the spirit. Sunlight and breeze playing among the leaves cast shadows and designs on the grass. The tree's shade makes a cool, lovely place to rest. *Lord, make my life a respite from the summer heat and fall storms.*
- Strengthen me—With roots growing deeper and branches waving higher, a tree is a picture of strength. Wild winds may bend and even break a few branches, but the tree remains firmly rooted. Scorching heat or rushing torrent leave the tree unshaken. *My heart cries out to you, O God. Increase my faith that I will graciously accept all the changes my losses bring.* Where there is true faith, change occurs graciously.
- Produce fruit in me—Producing fruit is the purpose of a tree's life. Fruit production is a channel of blessing to all. Is this not the purpose of my life? "Herein is my Father glorified, that ye bear much fruit" (John 15:8).

Lord, make me fruitful! Right now I feel like a dried up tree in a desert land. I am in a year of drought. But you brought me out of the valley and drought before, and you can do it again. Pour out upon me your refreshing showers. When I put my trust in you, you give me hope for more fruitful days ahead. Lord, boost my trust and hope in you. Provide sap for my growth.

QUESTIONS

1. In what ways do I need to grow?
2. How do I desire God to beautify me?
3. How have the hard things in my life made me more fruitful?
4. In what ways is my life productive?
5. In what ways is my life unproductive?

Peace, Perfect Peace

Peace I leave with you, my peace I give unto you: not as the world giveth, give I unto you. Let not your heart be troubled, neither let it be afraid. John 14:27

Peace to you—prosperity, health of soul, and serenity. This was the greeting Jesus and His followers gave to each other.

Peace is the power to hold the wildest fear in pause, to still the clamor of a questioning, anxious mind, or to hush the cry of a lacerated heart. Peace is mercy instead of damnation, hope instead of despair, and life instead of death.

In these words, "Peace I leave with you, the peace that is mine, I give to you," the love of a lifetime that lasts for eternity is condensed. Christ's legacy of peace is more valuable than anything anyone anywhere can offer us. Peace was Christ's last and best legacy that lives forever. It is a legacy of security, of identity, and of wellbeing.

Christ's peace is one that calms within while the storm rages without. It is peace of conscience, harmony with God, and love between humans. What is more precious than this treasure that we absolutely need and cannot do without?

Christ gives peace "not as the world gives." The world says, "Peace, peace," but there is war and hate. They say, "Peace," but their end is destruction. Those serving self and Satan know no peace because they do not have the inner relationship with Christ that brings peace. The world is powerless to give peace to the troubled heart.

Because of Christ's legacy of peace, we can obey His command, "Let not your heart be troubled" (John 14:1). Life is full of events, trials, and sorrows that can terrorize and traumatize our fainting hearts. Jesus knew those things were coming to His disciples, and He knew they would come to us as His followers. His promise of peace gave His disciples hope and strength to go on living and blessing others, and it can do the same for us today.

The secret of my peace lies in my faith in God and in my obedience to Him. The more I know Him and His almighty power and wisdom, the deeper and more stable my peace will be.

The sun will shine again. I will rejoice again in God's favor. Today sorrow colors my life; tomorrow God's favor colors my life; such is life on earth. *Lord, let me neither be presumptuous in sunshine nor despairing in the darkness.*

Peace is God's identifying mark on His people.

QUESTIONS

1. What is my personal definition of peace?
2. How have I felt peace in the middle of my storm?
3. What causes my inner turmoil?
4. Does God ever plan that His child be in a state of turmoil?
5. What causes me to lose my peace? How do I regain my peace?

For Want of a Word

The Lord GOD hath given me the tongue of the learned, that I should know how to speak a word in season to him that is weary: he wakeneth morning by morning, he wakeneth mine ear to hear as the learned. Isaiah 50:4

Lost for want of a word—
A word that you might have spoken!
Who knows what eyes may be dim,
Or what hearts may be aching and broken?
—author unknown

"The extent of our knowledge of God and of His truth is the measure of our power to influence and bless our fellow men. A man who is learning daily of God is a man who is daily gaining power to teach and help his brethren."[53]

The more we know, the more we are responsible to share. What are the hard things teaching me? Am I learning how to comfort the sad, cheer the weary, take time for the lonely, guide the perplexed, help the wavering, strengthen the faint, offer hope to the dying?

Oh, there is much I have learned, but so much more to learn. Am I going to open my heart to this challenge or will I back into a safe corner and close my ears to the cries of other hurting hearts? Do I feel like the widow who said, "I have so many difficulties and so many things I'm trying to work through, I have no strength of mind or body to reach out to someone else's pain"? Sometimes I am tempted to feel that I have been through so much pain that I do not want to hear the sorrows and groans of others. I have been through so much grief; my heart has no room for the tears and heartaches of another.

O Lord, spare me from such selfish thoughts. Soften and enlarge my heart for another's pain. Stabilize my mind and strengthen my thoughts to empathize with the anguish of another. Place words of wisdom and comfort on my lips. Grant me the ability to share what you are teaching me. Keep me aware of my privilege and responsibility.

Master, let me be a Braille transcription of thee that the blind may read and go seeing. Let the work of my hands be a sign language that the deaf and dumb may read and find their own songs. Let my feet walk in love beside the lame, who may find thy footprints to the Way. Let no man inquire of me: "Who art thou and whence comest thou?" Rather let me so live that men may ask: "Whose art thou and whither may I go to find Him?"

—Mary Welch

QUESTIONS

1. What do I have to share with other hurting hearts?
2. Is it necessary that I reach out to others who hurt? What do I think God would tell me?
3. When I reach into another's hurting heart, my own wound opens and I feel my pain and theirs. Yet hurting with and for someone else is a blessed way to heal my own pain. Explain if this is true for you. Tell how and why?

Don't Forfeit Your Inheritance

Wherefore thou art no more a servant, but a son; and if a son, then an heir of God through Christ. Galatians 4:7

As a child of God, I am heir of all that is good and blessed. I am an heir . . .
of liberty,
of truth,
of love,
of God Himself,
of His eternal kingdom.

What a wonderfully rich child of God I am, not because I possess decaying, mortal things, but because I have been given living, eternal riches! Nevertheless, there is the possible horror of forfeiting my inheritance. The danger is real; it can happen to any of us.

Some who have lost a loved one, or lost their health or wealth, or lost their position and reputation, or lost their purity and piety, have also lost their faith while in the valley. We want to avoid forfeiting our faith and inheritance at all costs. Let's beware of these forfeiting steps:

- Forfeit liberty—by becoming enslaved to doubts and bitter feelings, refusing to forgive or to accept forgiveness, and refusing to accept God's plan. When we insist on understanding God's ways or on retaining our bitterness, we lose our liberty to have faith and trust in Him or to be forgiven by Him.
- Forfeit truth—by believing the lies of Satan. "God has forsaken me," "God is punishing me," and "God does not care about me," are all lies of Satan. When we believe these lies, we do not believe God's Word. When God's Word loses credibility in our hearts, we become lost in the dark.
- Forfeit honor—by seeking comfort in the wrong place. Many hurting hearts turn to alcohol, drugs, sex, or other tools Satan uses to console. These counterfeits temporarily anesthetize the mind but destroy the body and the soul.

- Forfeit love—by failing to accept God's love. Poor choices often lead to broken relationships, limiting our ability to receive the love of God and others.
- Forfeit the friendship of Jesus. This is the terrible but natural outcome of the previous forfeitures. Christ can no longer walk with one who has chosen to leave His side. When we lose God's loving favor, we lose everything.
- Forfeit the hope of eternal life. When fidelity is lost, hope is lost also. When hope is lost, all is lost!

However, we must never forget that all can be regained when we turn to Jesus in repentance, surrender our lives, and renew our faith in Him. Hope and peace will follow.

QUESTIONS

1. What part of my inheritance am I forfeiting by my stubbornness?
2. Is my heavenly inheritance more important to me than my earthly inheritance?
3. What does being an heir of God mean to me?

Comfortable and Happy

Now our Lord Jesus Christ himself, and God, even our Father, which hath loved us, and hath given us everlasting consolation and good hope through grace, comfort your hearts, and stablish you in every good word and work. 2 Thessalonians 2:16–17

Some of humankind's strongest drives are to be comfortable and happy, to achieve inner peace, to find power to cope with life's hurdles, and to accomplish something of significance.

I am finding it difficult to be comfortable and happy since my losses. My inner peace is disturbed by internal chaos. Sometimes I feel weak and powerless to face life. My ability to perform has diminished. I need time to adjust after all the upheavals. Nevertheless, I ought to remember that my goal in life must not be to be comfortable and happy, but to be conformed to the will of God. Finding a new normal is all about the power of God and my acceptance of what has changed my life forever.

The blessing given in 2 Thessalonians is from our Lord Jesus Christ Himself. His divinity, His sacrifice, and His goodness give Him authority in heaven and on earth. He does not bless us as a master paying wages, but as a Father dealing lovingly and kindly with His children.

He has loved me in the past, He loves me now, and He will love me in the future—that is security, and that is comfort! Because of His love, He offers me comfort now and eternal comfort in the future. Because of His faithfulness, He offers me hope. Peace and hope are not choices, but they result from a choice. They are the result of my choice to place my trust in God. When I have faith in God, I find peace, and peace produces hope. So if I do not have peace or if I lack hope, I need faith in God.

When I am uncomfortable, not at peace, or writhing in grief, I am as unstable as water. Sorrow weakens. Sorrow distresses even the most trustful mind. Sorrow makes me unstable and unbalanced, putting me in great need of God's stabilizing comfort.

The breadth of divine comfort reaches every department of my life. Divine comfort offers a wider, fuller help than human comfort—help in every need of my body, soul, or spirit. Human comfort cannot do this. I must be careful not to expect too much from human consolation because it reaches only so deep.

Thank you, God, for your comfort that reaches into the vast hole of sorrow and extends hope even in the obscure hours of night.

Surrender to God's will is never a risk.

QUESTIONS

1. Is being comfortable and happy my goal in life? What makes me comfortable and happy?
2. What about my situation makes me uncomfortable and unhappy?
3. How is God's comfort different from human comfort?
4. How can I obtain and maintain peace and hope?

Growing Zone

Till we all come in the unity of the faith, and of the knowledge of the Son of God, unto a perfect man, unto the measure of the stature of the fulness of Christ: that we henceforth be no more children, tossed to and fro, and carried about with every wind of doctrine, by the sleight of men, and cunning craftiness, whereby they lie in wait to deceive; but speaking the truth in love, may grow up into him in all things, which is the head, even Christ. Ephesians 4:13–15

When God draws me out of my "comfort zone," He is directing me to a "growing zone." We tend to resent being pushed out of our comfort zone, but is that not the place where we grow and become strong? My spiritual vitality soon stagnates if I remain in my comfort zone too long. Comfort zones and growing zones simply do not overlap.

When I am uncomfortable and struggling, when I do not know the next step, when my place of comfort suddenly turns into pain, that is when I stretch my arms to God in effectual, fervent prayer. That is when I offer up my ways, my wisdom, and my independence, and I surrender to the power and wisdom of the Almighty.

Jesus Himself is the source of growth. We are to "grow up into Him in all things." As we grow in knowledge of Christ, we learn to speak the truth in love (v. 15). Of course, this is for the benefit of the believers with whom we worship—the church. But being able to speak the truth in love has great personal benefits also, for he who speaks the truth in love has experienced the gentle, stable character qualities of Christ and has become a full-grown individual. *O Lord, I have a long way to grow!*

As a person who is grieving, I really need to learn to speak the truth in love, even though it is much easier to protect myself with a false front. I find it especially difficult to share my true emotions with some people, while I share more easily with others. Yet that must not be uncommon or necessarily wrong, for even Jesus had His inner circle of disciples—Peter, James, and John—with whom He shared some special moments. He did not open up the view of His transfiguration to all of His disciples. He did not share the intensity of His pain in the garden with all of His followers. Yet He spoke the truth in love to everyone who sought His help.

I cry out to God for help when I am out of my comfort zone, knowing that growth can be the beautiful outcome of an ugly trial. *Thank you, God, for growing zones—painful and uncomfortable as they may be!*

Being uncomfortable sets me free to grow.

QUESTIONS

1. How do I respond when God takes me out of my comfort zone?
2. What makes a person easy to share with?
3. What growing pains am I dealing with right now?

Failed?
Try Again

And Simon answering said unto him, Master, we have toiled all the night, and have taken nothing: nevertheless at thy word I will let down the net. Luke 5:5

Have you ever "toiled all the night" and still ended up being a total failure? Peter and the other fishermen had failed to catch any fish. They had tried long and hard. Yet they had failed. However, when Jesus spoke, Peter replied, "Nevertheless at thy word I will let down the net."

That is where I am right now, Lord. I have tried so hard and failed so greatly that now, at your feet, I am crying for help and forgiveness.

Failure has displayed my weakness.
I come to you now, Lord, in meekness.

Failure has proved my unbelief.
I give to you my fears, seek relief.

Failure has taught me; I must trust
Not in self, but in God who is just.

Failures teach us many things about ourselves. I am too quick to speak my feelings. I am too quick to make rash judgments, too quick to speak of another's failures, even while squirming in my own. I have demanded justice for someone else while begging mercy for myself. I have been slow to give honest compliments.

I have learned much more about myself through my failures than through my successes. At times I have failed because I expected the Lord to do everything. Other times I have failed because I expected Him to do little.

Why did those fishermen fail? It was not because they were in the wrong spot, or they did not have the correct tackle. It was not because they had not tried hard enough. It was certainly not because they did not know how to fish. Did Jesus allow them to fail so they could experience the blessing of obedience even against common sense? Was He giving them a lesson in trust? Was Jesus asking them to cast aside their fishing knowledge and to have faith in Him? To swallow their pride and humbly cast the net on the other side?

O Lord, give me a heart of humble obedience. When you tell me where to fish, I must go to that spot and throw in the net. The rest of the work is yours.

The greatest accomplishment is not in never failing,
but in trying again after you fail.

—Vince Lombardi

QUESTIONS

1. What have my failures taught me about myself?
2. What has God asked me to do that is against common sense?
3. When I feel like a failure, how do I react? Am I quick to try again?

Be an Overcomer

He that hath an ear, let him hear what the Spirit saith unto the churches; To him that overcometh will I give to eat of the tree of life, which is in the midst of the paradise of God. Revelation 2:7

Life is a constant struggle. Life is war! In the natural and supernatural realms as well as in the physical, mental, moral, and spiritual areas, a constant battle rages.

The air I breathe to stay alive threatens to kill me with germs and pollutants.

My five senses, so necessary to enjoy the beauty of the world around me and to give me a well-rounded life, threaten to destroy me morally and physically, if I give in to my fleshly desires.

My thoughts can increase my knowledge and help me develop, grow, and mature, or they can destroy my mental balance and cause me to go insane. They can also destroy me spiritually with doubts and questions.

The spiritual food I feed on can assist in my growth to become more Christ-like, but false doctrine can confuse and drive me from God.

The battle is on!

- Am I aware there is a battle?
- What am I doing to keep myself fit for the fight physically, morally, mentally, and spiritually?
- What am I doing to keep from Satan's pitfalls?
- Am I feeding myself spiritually?
- What am I feeding into my mind?
- Am I an overcomer, or am I being overcome?
- What kind of books am I reading?
- What kind of music do I listen to?
- What kind of friends do I spend my time with?
- What is my goal in life?
- Whom have I chosen to be my Master? Do I live for myself, which is serving Satan, or for God?
- Have I surrendered my will to my Master?

How I wage this battle in my daily choices makes all the difference in this present world and in eternity.

QUESTIONS

1. Do I allow my senses to govern my behavior, or am I led by the Spirit?
2. Do I make wise or foolish daily choices?
3. In what ways am I aware of the battle that rages around me every day? Am I aware of Christ by my side?

Strength for the Battle

Enter ye in at the strait gate: for wide is the gate, and broad is the way, that leadeth to destruction, and many there be which go in thereat: because strait is the gate, and narrow is the way, which leadeth unto life, and few there be that find it. Matthew 7:13–14

Oswald Chambers said, "The Christian life is gloriously difficult, but its difficulty does not make us faint and cave in—it stirs us up to overcome."[54] I would add that the Christian life is excruciatingly, painfully difficult at times, and sometimes we do faint and need to be carried on the Good Shepherd's shoulders—and still it stirs us up to overcome!

Why do I keep fighting when the battle seems impossible?

Because . . .

- I know the abundance of His ability.
- I experience the bounty of His blessings.
- I find contentment in His care.
- I live in the fullness of His faithfulness.
- I trust the goodness of His grace.
- I know the joy of His justice.
- I see the light of His love.
- I experience a multitude of His mercies.
- I feel the peace of His presence.
- I rest in His reliability.
- I find strength in His stability.
- I trust in His truth.

When the battle rages, God cheers me on to be my best for His glory. He alone supplies the courage, determination, and holiness to move forward.

Oswald Chambers also said, "It takes a tremendous amount of discipline to live the worthy and excellent life of a disciple of Jesus in the realities of life."[55]

Help me, Lord, to view my trials as a part of that discipline you send to keep me in the narrow way. Since you were "made perfect (made complete, accomplished, fulfilled) through suffering," that must be the aim of any tribulation you might allow (Hebrews 5:8–9).

> There is never a river too deep,
> But He'll find a crossing.
> Never a mountain too steep,
> But He'll find a safe pass.
> There is never a storm so wild,
> But that His presence brings peace.
> There is never a trial so painful,
> But that His compassion brings release.

QUESTIONS

1. In what ways do I find the Christian battle difficult?
2. What encourages me to keep on fighting?
3. Do I ever feel like giving up in the battle? What causes those feelings of discouragement?
4. What promises does God give me that make the battle worth the struggle?
5. In what ways am I being made perfect through suffering?

Love in All Things

[Love] beareth all things, believeth all things, hopeth all things, endureth all things. 1 Corinthians 13:7

Larry Crabb said, "The mark of the Christian is a quality of love that directs more energy toward others' concerns than toward one's own wellbeing. Nominal Christians and unbelievers are capable of extraordinary acts of kindness, but only the trusting Christian can be more concerned with another's longings than with his own. Unfortunately, however, very few are. The church has lost its power because it loves so poorly."[56] How sadly true! Let's not get caught in the unlovely web of selfishness and self-protection. We all have experienced it, no doubt.

Does my hurting heart cause me to love more or less? Do my hard experiences cause me to take more notice of the difficulties of others? Do the longings in my heart prompt me to reach out to others who may have similar longings? In what ways should my Christian love manifest itself?

Do I choose to ache and wrap myself up in a self-protecting cover? Do I choose to sink in self-pity and nurse the snubs and cold shoulders offered me? Do I choose to withdraw from relationships because they are too risky?

Or do I have the love that "bears up under anything and everything that comes, is ever ready to believe the best of every person, its hopes are fadeless under all circumstances, and it endures everything [without weakening]"? (1 Corinthians 13:7, Amplified Bible, Classic Edition [AMPC][57]). That is the kind of love that never fails—never fades out or becomes obsolete or comes to an end.

What will I choose? Self-protection or trust? Self-pity or denial of pain? To withdraw or to reach out?

When we experience a major loss, we go through a time of feeling as if we are suffocating in our pain. We have no strength, no desire, and no ability to reach out to others. However, as we feel the healing touch of God in our pain, our hearts will be filled with love and gratitude. In time, we will have some lessons of great value to share with others. When we grow in the time of our grief, love will blossom and flow to others who need that loving touch and understanding word. Living with pain should expand our hearts to express love. The more we love, the more we feel pain. The more pain, the more we love. That is God's plan, but it is only fulfilled in the surrendered heart.

Faith, like light, should always be simple and unbending;
while love, like warmth, should beam forth on every side,
and bend to every necessity of our brethren.[58]

—Martin Luther

QUESTIONS

1. How has my church family responded to my troubled heart?
2. What has my hurting heart done for me positively or negatively?
3. I must remember that I can love God no more than the person I love the least. Does my love for God and others need to grow?
4. How would love help solve some of the emotions I am dealing with?

Rainbow Promise

I do set my bow in the cloud, and it shall be for a token of a covenant between me and the earth. And it shall come to pass, when I bring a cloud over the earth, that the bow shall be seen in the cloud: and I will remember my covenant, which is between me and you and every living creature of all flesh; and the waters shall no more become a flood to destroy all flesh. Genesis 9:13–15

God's promise of the rainbow came after the greatest disaster of all time. It came after the most massive loss ever endured by the human race. In fact, the entire human race was lost—except for eight godly souls.

Surely Noah and his family lost relatives and friends. Their hearts must have filled with grief when they saw the floodwaters rise. Noah had admonished, warned, and begged the people to repent—but no one listened to him. His message of love and hope was rejected.

I doubt that we can imagine what went through the hearts and minds of those few who safely rode out the deluge. I am sure they were thankful that they were safe, but they likely were hurting and sorrowing over all those who were lost in the flood. What must it have been like to begin a new life that included only their small family, all other friends and relatives gone?

Noah and his family probably did a lot of crying and praying on that boat ride. How would life go on? Nothing would ever be the same. They would have to make a new life in a new place. The devastation that they experienced would ever live in their minds. Yet, they chose to praise and thank the God who created the flood of destruction. They did not blame God for annihilating the rest of humanity. They knew God as a God of love, fairness, and justice. They found comfort, courage, and confidence in the knowledge that they were in the will of God.

When the waters finally receded and the family came out of the ark, their first act was one of sacrifice and praise. God responded with the beautiful bow of His eternal promise. "And it shall come to pass, when I bring a cloud over the earth, that the bow shall be seen in the cloud: and I will remember my covenant, which is between me and you and every living creature of all flesh; and the waters shall no more become a flood to destroy all flesh." *Thank you, Lord, for rainbows which remind us to praise you for your faithfulness and unchanging love in the storms of life.*

The flowers live by the tears that fall
From the sad face of the skies;
And life would have no joys at all,
Were there no watery eyes.

Love thou thy sorrow: grief shall bring
Its own excuse in after years;
The rainbow!—see how fair a thing
God hath built up from tears.[59]

—Henry Septimus Sutton

QUESTIONS

1. What brought Noah's family comfort?
2. What message do I receive from the rainbow? How does it give me hope?
3. What about the future seems scary to me?
4. Do I think the future seemed frightening to Noah's family? Why or why not?

Shortsighted

My days are past, my purposes are broken off, even the thoughts of my heart. They change the night into day: the light is short because of darkness. If I wait, the grave is mine house: I have made my bed in the darkness. Job 17:11–13

Job felt devoid of purpose. God had allowed Satan to take away everything he valued except his wife, leaving him sick of heart, diseased of body, and dismayed in mind. Job's life was beyond any hope, dreams, or goals. Life was over for him as far as he could see. There was no rhyme or reason to the painful turns in his life.

Life's circumstances had changed, he had changed, his friends and family had changed, and it seemed God had changed. (In reality, God never changes. His way of dealing with us may change, but God's attitude toward us is the same. He still loves us!) In his deepest, darkest moments, Job had no motivation to go on living. What he once had been, he no longer was. Only darkness and death awaited him.

Poor Job! How shortsighted he was to the purpose and plan of God. God had a completely new life planned for Job. God had proved his point to Satan. Job was His faithful and willing servant, not for what he could get from God, but because he knew and loved God in a personal way.

Ah! How often I find myself in Job's shoes. What good could possibly be ahead for me? Sadness, sickness, and death are all I see on the horizon.

Oh, me! How shortsighted I have been and still am! Yes, my life has changed drastically, but that does not mean it can never be good again. It is and will be different, but different is not always bad.

I am learning to live again, and although living is different, is it good because God is in the "different" with me. I am learning to dream again, but my dreams are much more realistic. I am learning to hope again, but my hopes are heavenly, not earthly.

The day is long and the day is hard,
I am tired of the march and keeping guard;
Tired of the sense of a fight to be won,
Of days to live through, and of work to be done;

The work which I count so hard to do,
He makes it easy, for He works too.
The days that are long belong to Him—
As He fills my sad heart with a sweet hymn.[60]

—J. R. Miller

QUESTIONS

1. Do I feel life is without purpose and over for me?
2. In what ways is my life different? Is it a good different or a painful different?
3. How have my experiences changed me from the person I once was?

Dwelling Place

Lord, thou hast been our dwelling place in all generations. Psalm 90:1

You have made us for yourself, O Lord,
and our heart is restless until it rests in you.[61]
—Augustine

How well I deal with my grief may depend to a great extent on my dwelling place. If I live in a house, my dwelling place is probably secure, relaxed, and comfortable. If I live in a cardboard box on the street, my dwelling place is very insecure, stressful, and uncomfortable. My dwelling place is where I live, not a place I visit now and then. My dwelling place should provide bodily comfort, mental security, and safety. Where is my soul dwelling? In the dark depths of sorrow and loss, or in the Lord? Am I dwelling in the gloom of self-pity, doubt, and despair, or in the light of His presence?

This psalm was written by Moses, who for forty years had had no fixed dwelling place. Yet he found God to be his dwelling place while he led the vast multitude of murmuring Israelites through the wilderness. Sometimes one or two people try our patience and cause us to long for a hiding place, but what about Moses and that massive crowd of problem-creating humanity? Moses found his hiding place in the Lord.

The Lord declares that He has been our dwelling place through all generations, but am I living in that dwelling place? God is our natural home, and we can never find rest until we find our rest in Him. "He that dwelleth in the secret place of the most High shall abide under the shadow of the Almighty. I will say of the LORD, He is my refuge and my fortress: my God; in him will I trust" (Psalm 91:1–2).

By faith I must make the Lord my dwelling place. The things I see, feel, smell, and taste in this world around me seem more tangible, more real, and more convincing than the reality of Him as my dwelling place. In this human body, the tangible is so much more powerful than the intangible.

Open my spiritual eyes, Lord, sensitize my spiritual longings that I might stay more connected to you and become more aware of the powerful spiritual world about me.

Difficult trials, difficult people, despairing circumstances bring the source of my security into sharp focus. When the tides of life suddenly change, when feelings of confusion and discouragement surge around me, when the waves of grief submerge me, where do I look for security?

- To a theory I have about God?
- To a position I feel God has given me?
- To another person?
- To an experience?
- To my feelings?

Theories, positions, people, experiences, and feelings all change. They are easily altered by the storms of life. Only God is reliable, constant, unmovable, unchanging, and trustworthy.

Lord, when you tell me to trust you at all times (Psalm 62:8), *I must reply, "I will trust, and not be afraid"* (Isaiah 12:2). *When you tell me to cast all my care upon you* (1 Peter 5:7), *I must reply, "I give you my burdens, Lord." When you say,* ***"Let not your heart be troubled"*** (John 14:1), *I must say, "I will not be anxious or worried." When you say,* ***"Abide in me"*** (John 15:4), *I must reply, "I will abide."*

O Lord, forgive my unbelief, my hesitation, my lack of confidence. I need you as my dwelling place, and you have promised to be there for me. Help me to live, to stay, and to settle in your dwelling place. Your eye is on the sparrow, so surely you care for me.

QUESTIONS

1. Where is my soul dwelling?
2. Do I feel secure, safe, and comfortable where I am right now?
3. How can I make and keep God as my dwelling place?

The Greatest Is Love

For now we see through a glass, darkly; but then face to face: now I know in part; but then shall I know even as also I am known. And now abideth faith, hope, charity, these three; but the greatest of these is charity. 1 Corinthians 13:12–13

Charity—love, my love for God—is the only bridge that will cross this great chasm of darkness. Love for God is the only viaduct across the gulf cut into my soul by life's pain and losses.

Love for God gives me strength to bear all things (1 Corinthians 13:7). Love is the strongest force in the soul; it is the strongest sustaining power of life. Love has upheld me through all of life's draining trials.

Love is the strongest resisting power. It supplies the impetus for resisting the temptations of fear, anger, and hopelessness. Love softens wrongs and suffering with a beautiful calmness and trust.

Love for God and others believes all things (1 Corinthians 13:7). Love thinks kind and forgiving thoughts of God and fellowmen, even when my heart is broken with sorrow. This love alone will keep me from casting blame on God and others. When my heart is soothed by blaming others for my pain, I am loving myself more than God or my fellowmen.

Love in my heart makes it easier to believe all things, to believe that even great losses and hurts will work out for my good. It reminds me that God really cares and that He has my good at heart. Love tells me that, "As for God, his way is perfect" (Psalm 18:30). He makes no mistakes!

Love also causes me to hope all things (1 Corinthians 13:7). Love and hope are sisters; they belong and work together. True hope persists when there is no evident reason to hope, when dreams are shattered, when the heart is wounded, when the body is in pain, or when the reputation is crushed. Hope is more than the result of a sanguine temperament. Hope is the gift of God's love and grace. It is an education in patience and faith. It holds back its fulfillment while expanding the soul's capacity for the fullest gratification. It looks above and beyond the sorrows and trials of this earth. It looks into the face of God and surrenders to His will; there it finds fulfillment. It supplies the patience and faith to endure all things (1 Corinthians 13:7). Through doubts and darkness, pain and trial, standing and waiting, hope endures.

O Lord, when the storms of life threaten to take me under, increase my love that bears all things, believes all things, hopes all things, and endures all things.

QUESTIONS

1. What are some of the "all things" that love has helped me with throughout my lifetime?
2. In what ways do I show love to my family?
3. In what ways do I show love to God?
4. What are some of the ways God shows love to me?
5. In what ways have my grief and trials brought more love into my life?

Appendix A
Who Is God?

A. W. Tozer said, "What you think about God is the most important thing about you!"[62] What we think about God will determine our attitude toward life and toward the blessings and pain that come our way. What we think about God will bring us comfort, contentment, and hope; or worry, bitterness, and despair.

God's attributes are not isolated traits of His character, but facets of His whole being—aspects of a perfect whole.

God has many more attributes than those listed. We can add to this list the qualities we have found in God. As we go through difficult, excruciating experiences, we must bring God's attributes into sharp focus. When we remember who God is, our questions, our stress, our worry, our fears, our trying to control will fade into the fullness of His greatness, power, and compassion. We must lay aside our thoughts—limited by time and space—our designs and desires, our preconceived ideas and plans, and let God be God!

INCOMPREHENSIBLE

God cannot be described in human language! God is incomprehensible to the human mind. God cannot be reduced to human terms.

In his description of God, Ezekiel uses the words *like, as, likeness, as it were,* to help create a mental picture (Ezekiel 1:27).

"Canst thou by searching find out God? canst thou find out the Almighty unto perfection? It is as high as heaven; what canst thou do? deeper than hell; what canst thou know? The measure thereof is longer than the earth, and broader than the sea" (Job 11:7–9).

SELF-EXISTENT

God has no origin;[63] He simply always was, is, and will be. Because God is, I am. No God, no man. No God, no earth. No God, no anything!

"And God said unto Moses, I AM THAT I AM: and he said, Thus shalt thou say unto the children of Israel, I AM hath sent me unto you" (Exodus 3:14).

"I am Alpha and Omega, the beginning and the end, the first and the last" (Revelation 22:13).

SELF-SUFFICENT

All life is in and from God. Nothing and no one is necessary to God. God has no needs; all our needs are met in Him. There is nothing necessary to God's existence; He is the necessity of our existence.

"For as the Father hath life in himself; so hath he given to the Son to have life in himself" (John 5:26).

"For in him we live, and move, and have our being" (Acts 17:28).

ETERNAL

God is everlasting, without a beginning, without an ending. The contrast between "God's eternity and man's mortality ought to convince us that faith in Jesus Christ is not optional."[64]

"The eternal God is thy refuge, and underneath are the everlasting arms" (Deuteronomy 33:27).

INFINITE

When we serve an infinite God, we can expect Him to surprise us, to astonish us, to overwhelm us, and to transcend us. When we try to calculate His next move, we pull Him down to our understanding. The infinite God will not fit into our brain and will defy our human understanding. Everything about God is without limitation.

- Love without measure. "For God so loved the world, that he gave his only begotten Son, that whosoever believeth in him should not perish, but have everlasting life" (John 3:16).
- Mercy and truth eternal. "For the LORD is good; his mercy is everlasting; and his truth endureth to all generations" (Psalm 100:5).
- Thoughts without number. "How precious also are thy thoughts unto me, O God! how great is the sum of them!" (Psalm 139:17).
- Boundless grace. "Moreover the law entered, that the offence might abound. But where sin abounded, grace did much more abound" (Romans 5:20).

IMMUTABLE

God is unchangeable. "He never differs from Himself."[65] He cannot change for the better because He is perfect. God can never change for the worse. "All that God is, He has always been; and all that He has been and is, He will ever be."[66]

"Jesus Christ the same yesterday, and to day, and for ever" (Hebrews 13:8).

"For I am the LORD, I change not; therefore ye sons of Jacob are not consumed" (Malachi 3:6).

OMNISCIENT

God possesses perfect knowledge and needs to learn nothing![67] I can neither inform Him of anything nor hide anything from Him.

"Who hath directed the Spirit of the LORD, or being his counsellor hath taught him?" (Isaiah 40:13).

"Hast thou not known? hast thou not heard, that the everlasting God, the LORD, the Creator of the ends of the earth, fainteth not, neither is weary? there is no searching of his understanding" (Isaiah 40:28).

WISE

"Wisdom, among other things, is the ability to devise perfect ends and to achieve those ends by the most perfect means."[68] God sees the end from the beginning! He sees everything in focus in relation to everything else. "All God's acts are done in perfect wisdom."[69]

"O the depth of the riches both of the wisdom and knowledge of God! how unsearchable are his judgments, and his ways past finding out!" (Romans 11:33).

OMNIPOTENT

God has all power. He is almighty. Nothing is too hard for Him.

"God hath spoken once; twice have I heard this; that power belongeth unto God" (Psalm 62:11).

He promises His power to His people. "But they that wait upon the LORD shall renew their strength; they shall mount up with wings as eagles; they shall run, and not be weary; and they shall walk, and not faint" (Isaiah 40:31).

TRANSCENDENT

Exalted far above the created universe—not in physical distance, but in His quality of being. Therefore, we must worship and serve God with reverence and fear. God is awesome and dreadful.

"And one cried unto another, and said, Holy, holy, holy, is the LORD of hosts: the whole earth is full of his glory. Then said I, Woe is me! for I am undone; because I am a man of unclean lips, and I dwell in the midst of a people of unclean lips" (Isaiah 6:3, 5).

OMNIPRESENT

God is here, God is everywhere. "God is close to everything and everyone."[70] God is with me in every circumstance, every pain, every trial, every joy.

". . . and, lo, I am with you alway, even unto the end of the world. Amen" (Matthew 28:20).

"Whither shall I go from thy spirit? or whither shall I flee from thy presence?

If I ascend up into heaven, thou art there: if I make my bed in hell, behold, thou art there. If I take the wings of the morning, and dwell in the uttermost parts of the sea; even there shall thy hand lead me, and thy right hand shall hold me" (Psalm 139:7–10).

FAITHFUL

God is immutable because He is faithful. He is faithful because He is immutable. He is ever true to His Word.

"Faithful is he that calleth you, who also will do it" (1 Thessalonians 5:24).

"Great is thy faithfulness" (Lamentations 3:23).

GOOD

All our daily blessings come from the goodness of God. There is no merit in human conduct, prayer, or faith. When we repent, God forgives because of His goodness. When we pray, God hears because He is good. Our expression of faith is simply confidence in God's goodness. "God's greatness causes fear to rise within us, but His goodness encourages us not to be afraid."[71]

"Thou crownest the year with thy goodness; and thy paths drop fatness" (Psalm 65:11).

"Or despisest thou the riches of his goodness and forbearance and longsuffering; not knowing that the goodness of God leadeth thee to repentance?" (Romans 2:4).

JUST

"Judgment is the application of justice to moral situations."[72] When God judges, "He simply acts like Himself from within. He is influenced by nothing outside Himself."[73] His judgments are just and right because of who He is.

"Lift up thyself, thou judge of the earth: render a reward to the proud" (Psalm 94:2).

"In the day when God shall judge the secrets of men by Jesus Christ according to my gospel" (Romans 2:16).

MERCIFUL

Mercy is the unlimited and inexhaustible ability of God to be compassionate. Human misery and sin call forth God's divine mercy to shine in our dark night.

"But the mercy of the LORD is from everlasting to everlasting upon them that fear him, and his righteousness unto children's children" (Psalm 103:17).

GRACIOUS

The good pleasure of God that inclines Him to bestow benefits upon the undeserving. The unlimited and unmerited favor of God.

"And he said unto me, My grace is sufficient for thee: for my strength is made perfect in weakness. Most gladly therefore will I rather glory in my infirmities, that the power of Christ may rest upon me" (2 Corinthians 12:9).

"For by grace are ye saved through faith; and that not of yourselves: it is the gift of God" (Ephesians 2:8).

LOVING

Love is an essential attribute of God. God's love is unchanging, uncaused, and undeserved.

"For God so loved the world, that he gave his only begotten Son, that whosoever believeth in him should not perish, but have everlasting life" (John 3:16).

HOLY

God is pure, sinless to the highest degree. To the natural man, holiness is incomprehensible, unapproachable, and unattainable. Holiness is the way to God. Holiness is His standard. Not until we realize God's holiness will we see our personal depravity.

"Sanctify yourselves therefore, and be ye holy: for I am the LORD your God" (Leviticus 20:7).

SOVEREIGN

God's sovereign rule encompasses all of creation. To be sovereign God must be all-knowing, all-powerful, and absolutely free to carry out His eternal purposes in every detail.

"Thus saith the LORD the King of Israel, and his redeemer the LORD of hosts; I am the first, and I am the last; and beside me there is no God" (Isaiah 44:6).

"And he said unto me, It is done. I am Alpha and Omega, the beginning and the end. I will give unto him that is athirst of the fountain of the water of life freely" (Revelation 21:6)

Appendix B

SEVEN CAUSES OF STAGNATION IN GRIEF

1. I have nothing left to be enthusiastic about.
2. I have allowed the pain in my heart to numb my mind and will.
3. I am not ready to move out of this valley.
4. I am painfully comfortable in my grief.
5. I cannot forgive, forget, or free myself from what I perceive as wrong.
6. I can never be truly happy again.
7. I am ready to quit; life seems too painful to go on.

SEVEN STEPS TO REVITALIZATION

1. Rejoice in the Lord—about something.
2. Pray without ceasing.
3. In everything give thanks.
4. Do not extinguish the Spirit.
5. Do not despise what God reveals.
6. Test all things against the truth.
7. Hold fast to that which is good.

—1 Thessalonians 5:16–21

Endnotes

[1] Larry Crabb, *Inside Out,* NavPress, Colorado Springs, 1988, p. 98.

[2] Karol Kuhn Truman, *Feelings Buried Alive Never Die . . .*, Olympus Distributing, Phoenix, 2003.

[3] Lettie Cowman and James Reimann, *Streams in the Desert: 366 Daily Devotional Readings,* Zondervan Publishing House, Grand Rapids, 1997, pp. 207–208.

[4] Ibid.

[5] H. D. M. Spence-Jones, Joseph S. Exell, and Edward Mark Deems, *The Pulpit Commentary*, Wm. B. Eerdmans Publishing Co., Grand Rapids, 1950.

[6] Christine Jette, "Shadow Grief," <http://www.thegrievingheart.info/shadowgrief.html>, accessed on June 15, 2016.

[7] W. G. Scroggie, *A Guide to the Psalms,* Kregel Publications, Grand Rapids, 1995, p. 77.

[8] George Horace Lorimer, *Letters from a Self-Made Merchant to His Son,* Outerbridge & Dienstfrey, New York, 1970.

[9] *The Christian Hymnal,* "Never Alone," No. 534.

[10] Larry Crabb, *Inside Out,* NavPress, Colorado Springs, 1988, p. 114.

[11] Ibid., p. 115.

[12] Ibid., p. 113.

[13] Hialmer Day Gould and Edward Louis Hessenmueller, *Best Thoughts of Best Thinkers, Amplified, Classified, Exemplified, and Arranged as a Key to Unlock the Literature of All Ages,* Best Thoughts Publishing Company, Cleveland, 1904, p. 434.

[14] Viktor E. Frankl, *Man's Search for Meaning,* Beacon Press, Boston, 2006.

[15] Tryon Edwards, *A Dictionary of Thoughts; Being a Cyclopedia of Laconic Quotations from the Best Authors of the World, Both Ancient and Modern,* F.B. Dickerson Co., Detroit, 1906, p. 361.

[16] Don Colbert, *Deadly Emotions: Understand the Mind-Body-Spirit Connection That Can Heal or Destroy You,* Thomas Nelson, Nashville, 2003, Chapter 1.

[17] Ibid.

[18] Ibid., p. 182.

[19] Nicholas Brady, Nahum Tate, Benjamin Edes, John Gill, Joshua Winter, Thomas Johnston, and Isaac Watts, *A New Version of the Psalms of David Fitted to the Tunes Used in Churches,* B. Edes and J. Gill, Boston, 1755.

[20] "Sometime We'll Understand," No. 496, *Favorite Hymns of Praise,* Tabernacle Publishing Co, Chicago, 1967.

[21] Larry Crabb, *Inside Out,* NavPress, Colorado Springs, 1988, p. 155.

[22] H. D. M. Spence-Jones, Joseph S. Exell, and Edward Mark Deems, *The Pulpit Commentary,* Wm. B. Eerdmans Publishing Co., Grand Rapids, 1950, Vol. 9, p. 117.

[23] Andrew Murray, *The Holiest of All,* Whitaker House, Springdale, PA, 1996.

[24] Josiah Conder, "How Shall I Follow Him I Serve?" *The Star in the East,* Chadwyck-Healey, Cambridge, England, 1992. Online at <http://uclibs.org/PID/52567>.

[25] H. D. M. Spence-Jones, Joseph S. Exell, and Edward Mark Deems, *The Pulpit Commentary,* Wm. B. Eerdmans Publishing Co., Grand Rapids, 1950, Vol. 1, p. 189.

[26] R. Tuck, "The Starting-Point of Human Wisdom," H. D. M. Spence-Jones, Joseph S. Exell, and Edward Mark Deems, *The Pulpit Commentary,* Wm. B. Eerdmans Publishing Co., Grand Rapids, 1950, Vol. 4, p. 42.

[27] Elisabeth Elliot, "Help Me Not to Want So Much," *The Path of Loneliness: Finding Your Way Through the Wilderness to God,* Vine Books, Ann Arbor, MI, 2001.

[28] Jeremiah 10:24, *World English Bible,* Christian Classics Ethereal Library, Grand Rapids, 2002.

[29] C. Short, "The Thunderstorm," H. D. M. Spence-Jones, Joseph S. Exell, and Edward Mark Deems, *The Pulpit Commentary,* Wm. B. Eerdmans Publishing Co., Grand Rapids, 1950, Vol. 4, p. 217.

[30] Tryon Edwards, *Useful Quotations,* Grosset and Dunlap Publishers, New York, 1933, p. 349.

[31] Tryon Edwards, *A Dictionary of Thoughts; Being a Cyclopedia of Laconic Quotations from the Best Authors of the World, Both Ancient and Modern,* F.B. Dickerson Co., Detroit, 1906, p. 11.

[32] H. D. M. Spence-Jones, Joseph S. Exell, and Edward Mark Deems, *The Pulpit Commentary,* Wm. B. Eerdmans Publishing Co., Grand Rapids, 1950, Vol. 6, p. 14.

[33] Charles Noel Douglas, *Forty Thousand Quotations, Prose and Poetical; Choice Extracts on History, Science, Philosophy, Religion, Literature, Etc. Selected from the Standard Authors of Ancient and Modern Times, Classified According to Subject,* G. Sully and Company, New York, 1917, p. 1198.

[34] A. W. Tozer, *The Knowledge of the Holy: The Attributes of God, Their Meaning in the Christian Life,* Harper & Row, New York, 1961, p. 60.

[35] Ibid., p. 60.

[36] Gerhard Tersteegen, Heinrich Seuse, and Frances A. Bevan, *Hymns of Ter Steegen, Suso, and Others,* Christian Classics Ethereal Library, Grand Rapids, 1990.

[37] John Greenleaf Whittier, *Hymns for Church and Home,* American Unitarian Association, Boston, 1904, p. 215.

[38] Bob Overton, "He Maketh No Mistake," <http://www.churchlead.com/mind_wanderings/view/1630/he_maketh_no_mistake#sthash.98j6yWy9.dpuf>, accessed on June 15, 2016.

[39] H. D. M. Spence-Jones, Joseph S. Exell, and Edward Mark Deems, *The Pulpit Commentary,* Wm. B. Eerdmans Publishing Co., Grand Rapids, 1950.

[40] George Rawlinson, Eustace R. Conder, and W. Clarkson, *Psalms,* Funk & Wagnalls, London, 1913, p. 9.

[41] Gerald L. Sittser, *A Grace Disguised,* Zondervan Publishing House, Grand Rapids, 1997, pp. 45–46.

[42] William J. Gaither, "We Have This Moment Today," 1975, accessed at <http://www.allthelyrics.com/lyrics/gaither_vocal_band/we_have_this_moment_today-lyrics-318634.html>.

[43] J. M. Barrie and Nora S. Unwin, *Peter Pan,* Charles Scribner's Sons, New York, 1950.

[44] As quoted in "Psalm 73:28," H. D. M. Spence-Jones, Joseph S. Exell, and Edward Mark Deems, *The Pulpit Commentary,* Wm. B. Eerdmans Publishing Co., Grand Rapids, 1950, Vol. 4, p. 80.

[45] H. D. M. Spence-Jones, Joseph S. Exell, and Edward Mark Deems, *The Pulpit Commentary,* Wm. B. Eerdmans Publishing Co., Grand Rapids, 1950, p. 358.

[46] Samuel Macauley Jackson, *Life and Character of Gerhard Tersteegen with Selections from His Letters and Writings,* William Allan, London, 1846, p. 128.

[47] Larry Crabb, *Inside Out,* NavPress, Colorado Springs, 1988, p. 114.

[48] Ibid., p. 144.

[49] Henry Ward Beecher and Edna Dean Proctor, *Life Thoughts: Gathered from the Extemporaneous Discourses of Henry Ward Beecher,* Phillips, Sampson and Co, Boston, 1858.

[50] As quoted in "Isaiah 50:7," H. D. M. Spence-Jones, Joseph S. Exell, and Edward Mark Deems, *The Pulpit Commentary,* Wm. B. Eerdmans Publishing Co., Grand Rapids, 1950, Vol. 5, p. 256.

[51] Horatius Bonar, "All That I Was," *The Bible Hymn-Book,* R. Carter & Bros., New York, 1860, p. 219, <http://catalog.hathitrust.org/api/volumes/oclc/38723811.html>, accessed on June 15, 2016.

[52] *Common Praise: Psalms, Hymns and Spiritual Songs for Use in the Church of England,* Christian Book Society, London, 1879, p. 309.

[53] H. D. M. Spence-Jones, Joseph S. Exell, and Edward Mark Deems, *The Pulpit Commentary,* Wm. B. Eerdmans Publishing Co., Grand Rapids, 1950, Vol. 5, p. 253.

[54] Oswald Chambers, *My Utmost for His Highest: Selections for the Year,* Barbour and Co, Uhrichsville, Ohio, 1991, p. 189.

[55] Ibid.

[56] Larry Crabb, *Inside Out,* NavPress, Colorado Springs, 1988, p. 107.

[57] *The Amplified Bible: Containing the Amplified Old Testament and the Amplified New Testament,* Zondervan Publishing House, Grand Rapids, 1965..

[58] Josiah H Gilbert, *Dictionary of Burning Words of Brilliant Writers: A Cyclopædia of Quotations from the Literature of All Ages,* W.B. Ketcham, New York, 1895.

[59] Henry Septimus Sutton, "The Flowers Live by the Tears," in Alfred H. Miles (ed.), *The Sacred Poets of the Nineteenth Century,* George Routledge & Sons, London, 1907.

[60] Albert Dieffenbach (ed.), *The Christian Register,* Christian Register Inc., Boston, 1919, Vol. 98, p. 279.

[61] Aurelius Augustinus, *St. Augustine's Confessions, (Lib 1,1-2,2.5,5: CSEL 33, 1-5),* Paris, 1638.

[62] A. W. Tozer, *The Knowledge of the Holy: The Attributes of God, Their Meaning in the Christian Life,* Harper & Row, New York, 1961, p. 1.

[63] Novatianus, *The Treatise of Novatian on the Trinity,* translated by Herbert Moore, London, New York, 1919, p. 25.

[64] A. W. Tozer, *The Knowledge of the Holy: The Attributes of God, Their Meaning in the Christian Life,* Harper & Row, New York, 1961, p. 42.

[65] Ibid., p. 49.

[66] Ibid.

[67] Ibid., p. 55.

[68] Ibid., p. 60.

[69] Ibid.

[70] Ibid., p. 74.

[71] Ibid., p. 84.

[72] Ibid., p. 87.

[73] Ibid., p. 86.

About the Author

After living in a house full of children and activity, Faythelma lives alone since her husband of forty-seven years passed away in 2008. They raised a family of nine and cared for over thirty children and adults in the beautiful hills of Estacada, Oregon.

Faythelma has been writing for over forty years. She did freelancing for twelve years, selling poetry, stories, and articles to religious magazines and Sunday school papers. She has also written junior Sunday school quarterlies for Christian Light Publications.

Books written by Faythelma are *Speedy Spanish Levels 1–3, Christian Ethics for Youth, School Days Devotional Praise, I Will Pass Over You, Sharpen UP, Reflections of God's Grace in Grief,* and *Light Through the Dark Valley.* She compiled four Creative Touch bulletin board books for teachers and reprinted *Inspiration for Education.*

Faythelma welcomes responses from her readers and invites you to email her at becbooks4u@gmail.com. You may also write to her in care of Christian Aid Ministries, P.O. Box 360, Berlin, Ohio, 44610.

Christian Aid Ministries

Christian Aid Ministries was founded in 1981 as a nonprofit, tax-exempt 501(c)(3) organization. Its primary purpose is to provide a trustworthy and efficient channel for Amish, Mennonite, and other conservative Anabaptist groups and individuals to minister to physical and spiritual needs around the world. This is in response to the command ". . . do good unto all men, especially unto them who are of the household of faith" (Galatians 6:10).

Each year, CAM supporters provide approximately 15 million pounds of food, clothing, medicines, seeds, Bibles, Bible story books, and other Christian literature for needy people. Most of the aid goes to orphans and Christian families. Supporters' funds also help to clean up and rebuild for natural disaster victims, put up Gospel billboards in the U.S., support several church-planting efforts, operate two medical clinics, and provide resources for needy families to make their own living. CAM's main purposes for providing aid are to help and encourage God's people and bring the Gospel to a lost and dying world.

CAM has staff, warehouses, and distribution networks in Romania, Moldova, Ukraine, Haiti, Nicaragua, Liberia, and Israel. Aside from management, supervisory personnel, and bookkeeping operations, volunteers do most of the work at CAM locations. Each year, volunteers at our warehouses, field bases, Disaster Response Services projects, and other locations donate over 200,000 hours of work.

CAM's ultimate purpose is to glorify God and help enlarge His kingdom. ". . . whatsoever ye do, do all to the glory of God" (1 Corinthians 10:31).

The Way to God and Peace

We live in a world contaminated by sin. Sin is anything that goes against God's holy standards. When we do not follow the guidelines that God our Creator gave us, we are guilty of sin. Sin separates us from God, the source of life.

Since the time when the first man and woman, Adam and Eve, sinned in the Garden of Eden, sin has been universal. The Bible says that we all have "sinned and come short of the glory of God" (Romans 3:23). It also says that the natural consequence for that sin is eternal death, or punishment in an eternal hell: "Then when lust hath conceived, it bringeth forth sin: and sin, when it is finished, bringeth forth death" (James 1:15).

But we do not have to suffer eternal death in hell. God provided forgiveness for our sins through the death of His only Son, Jesus Christ. Because Jesus was perfect and without sin, He could die in our place. "For God so loved the world that he gave his only begotten Son, that whosoever believeth in him should not perish, but have everlasting life" (John 3:16).

A sacrifice is something given to benefit someone else. It costs the giver greatly. Jesus was God's sacrifice. Jesus' death takes away the penalty of sin for everyone who accepts this sacrifice and truly repents of their sins. To repent of sins means to be truly sorry for and turn away from the things we have done that have violated God's standards (Acts 2:38; 3:19).

Jesus died, but He did not remain dead. After three days, God's Spirit miraculously raised Him to life again. God's Spirit does something similar in us. When we receive Jesus as our sacrifice and repent of our sins, our hearts are changed. We become spiritually alive! We develop new desires and attitudes (2 Corinthians 5:17). We begin to make choices that please God (1 John 3:9). If we do fail and commit sins, we can ask God for forgiveness. "If we confess our sins, he is faithful and just to forgive us our sins, and to cleanse us from all unrighteousness" (1 John 1:9).

Once our hearts have been changed, we want to continue growing spiritually. We will be happy to let Jesus be the Master of our lives and will want to become more like Him. To do this, we must meditate on God's Word and commune with God in prayer. We will testify to others of this change by being baptized and sharing the good news of God's victory over sin and death. Fellowship with a faithful group of believers will strengthen our walk with God (1 John 1:7).